Praise for
Hear No Evil

"Like a good Amy Grant song, *Hear No Evil* will worm its way into your brain, lodge itself there, and refuse to leave. Every page is funny, honest, and full of the best kind of faith. Matthew Paul Turner isn't just a great Christian writer. He's a great writer, period."

—KEVIN ROOSE, author of *The Unlikely Disciple: A Sinner's Semester at America's Holiest University*

"The most glorious part about *Hear No Evil* is Matthew Paul Turner's humor and authenticity. Brilliantly affective, this collection of stories about music—its triumphs, its dysfunction, and its value in people's lives—will conjure up memories about your own musical journey and experiences. Matthew's funny and sometimes irreverent tone reveals not only his social relevance but also his sincerity."

—JOSH SHIPP, host of *Jump Shipp*, author of *The Teen's Guide to World Domination*, MTV personality

"There's an adage: 'Never make fun of a group of which you are not a member.' Matthew Paul Turner grew up in the fundamentalist bubble and worked in the Christian Contemporary Music scene. And make fun of them he does—however, not with outsider venom but with insider empathy. *Hear No Evil* is hilarious, cringe-worthy, and all too true. And Turner's faith survived. Hallelujah. That's what humor can do."

—SUSAN E. ISAACS, actress, comedienne, and author of *Angry Conversations with God*

"*Hear No Evil* is a compelling story that will send you on a journey where you're laughing one second and doing a painfully honest heart check the next. When you finish this book you'll have a new understanding that God works in very unique and surprising ways as He draws us closer to Him."

—PETE WILSON, pastor of Cross Point Church, author of *Plan B*

"Anyone who grew up in the evangelical bubble will relive their own adolescence through Turner's witty, devastatingly forthright account of his own. Couching his unsparing observation in self-effacing mirth, he drags the superstition and cultural backwardness of the good ol' Christian subculture right out into the open. Even if you've had bad experiences with exorcisms in the past, *Hear No Evil* is the last one you'll ever need."

—DAVID SESSIONS, founding editor of *Patrol* magazine

"In *Hear No Evil* Matthew Paul Turner writes, 'The odd thing about Christians pursuing fame is that they do it while pretending not to be interested in fame.' I would buy this book even if this was the only sentence printed inside. It's that valuable."

—JONATHAN ACUFF, creator of StuffChristiansLike.net and author of the book *Stuff Christians Like*

Hear No Evil

My Story of
Innocence, Music,
and the
Holy Ghost

Matthew Paul Turner

WaterBrook
PRESS

HEAR NO EVIL
PUBLISHED BY WATERBROOK PRESS
12265 Oracle Boulevard, Suite 200
Colorado Springs, Colorado 80921

Scripture quotations are taken or paraphrased from the King James Version.

Details in some anecdotes and stories have been changed to protect the identities of the persons involved.

ISBN 978-1-4000-7472-3
ISBN 978-0-307-45853-7 (electronic)

Published in the United States by WaterBrook Multnomah, an imprint of the Crown Publishing Group, a division of Random House Inc., New York.

WATERBROOK and its deer colophon are registered trademarks of Random House Inc.

Library of Congress Cataloging-in-Publication Data
Turner, Matthew Paul, 1973–
    Hear no evil : my story of innocence, music, and the holy ghost / Matthew Paul Turner.—
1st ed..
        p. cm.
      ISBN 978-1-4000-7472-3 — ISBN 978-0-307-45853-7 (electronic)
    1. Music—Religious aspects—Christianity. 2. Turner, Matthew Paul, 1973– 3. Christian life.
I. Title.
    ML3921.2.T87 2010
    277.3'082092—dc22
    [B]

                                    2009041856

Printed in the United States of America
2010—First Edition

10 9 8 7 6 5 4 3 2 1

SPECIAL SALES
Most WaterBrook Multnomah books are available at special quantity discounts when purchased in bulk by corporations, organizations, and special-interest groups. Custom imprinting or excerpting can also be done to fit special needs. For information, please e-mail SpecialMarkets@WaterBrook-Multnomah.com or call 1-800-603-7051.

For Jessica and Elias

Contents

"Music and rhythm find their way into
the secret places of the soul."

—PLATO

Overture

Today the atmosphere at Fido, a coffeehouse in Nashville's midtown, is the same as it always is: moody, overcast, an almost cliché backdrop for creative people.

I'm here working, soaking up the scene, hoping to find an idea or the beginning of an idea that I can turn into a feature or an Op-Ed for one of Nashville's entertainment newspapers. I like this part of my job, one that simply requires me to watch, listen, drink coffee, and jot down notes on my laptop.

Two tables to my left, a twenty-something female holds a square piece of charcoal. She keeps looking up at two gentlemen sitting against the window, and then down at her sketch pad, practicing her skill at capturing the human form. Her subjects, each wearing a different vanity T-shirt, talk about technology and graphic design. At one point I hear one of them yell at a four-top in the corner of the coffeehouse. The only girl at the table yells back, asking if he's coming to their show on Friday evening. He shrugs. She pretends to be offended.

The majority of people sitting around me are singers, musicians, or wannabe singers or musicians. And most aren't the kind who fiddle, slide their guitars, or sing nasally on purpose. Well, the two fifty-ish men sitting at the booth across the way look like washed-up fiddlers, but Nashville's music scene has grown deep and wide since the first time I moved here in 1993. Country is still the mainstay of the music business here, but these days lots of people come to Nashville to pursue careers in rock, folk, jazz, blues, gospel, and Christian music, among other genres. Dreams of success draw many interesting people to Nashville—people full of life, passion, story, rage, opinion, and belief. And once in a while, talent.

A young man pushes through the front door, appearing lost, or perhaps hoping to be found. His expression is common here in Nashville, a nervous passion that tends to make talented people look socially misplaced. This man looks particularly out of his element. His eyes move around the room like two gerbils looking for an escape from their cage. I try to watch inconspicuously but fail when our eyes meet. Usually I feel embarrassed when I'm caught ogling strangers, but not this time. He clearly wants people to notice him.

It seems to me he woke up and conspired to put together a "look" that would attract attention: the tight black jeans, a multicolored T-shirt that shimmers in direct sunlight, a skinny black tie, and a purple vest are only the beginning of why he stands out. His hair is unnaturally shiny, dyed a color between blue and black, and shaped into six perfectly formed horns that jet out from his head in various directions. The eyeliner brings his look together, and for me, confirms the possibility that he's the love child of Boy George and Beetlejuice.

I'm not culturally ignorant; I realize a lot of people look like this guy. But he catches my attention because it isn't a typical fashion statement for people hanging out at Fido or any place else in Nashville at eight thirty in the morning—at least not without signs of a hangover.

It occurs to me that he and I might share one thing in common: neither of us looks like we belong at Fido. Most of the "creatives" who frequent this hangout are hipsters looking for their morning cup of coffee and free wireless. I wish I was cool enough to consider myself a hipster, but rather than make music, I mostly write about the hipsters who make it. Furthermore, I don't wear corduroy in the summer or shop weekly at the local farmers' market, and my wife, Jessica, says I look ridiculous in a fedora. And trust me, I try one on every time I shop at Target.

Out of the corner of my eye, I see the young man walking toward me.

"Excuse me," he says, "are you David?" He tosses a legal pad on the table next to mine and straightens his thin black tie. "I'm *Adam*." He says his name like he anticipates it being familiar.

"No, my name is Matthew. Sorry."

Glancing around the coffeehouse, Adam spins with all the drama of a model at the end of a catwalk. He sighs, plops down in a chair, and pulls his cell phone out of his pocket so he can use the screen as a mirror to check his eyeliner.

Shutting his phone with one hand, he says, "Can I just vent for a moment? It has been quite a morning—wow!"

I fear this could be the beginning of a lengthy conversation, and I wonder if it would be rude to remind him that I'm not David.

"And you know what?" he continues. "I'm actually relieved you're not the fellow I'm supposed to meet. This meeting is important, and I was so afraid that I was late. My taxi arrived fifteen minutes later than scheduled. But I guess he's late too."

I look up from my computer and smile slightly, a polite gesture so he doesn't feel like he's talking to himself. I don't mean it to be an invitation for chitchat. However, my good manners lead Adam to ask if I mind watching his legal pad and pen while he stands in line for a drink.

"That's fine," I say.

Adam returns to his table a few minutes later with a hot drink in his hand. He looks at his watch, mumbles to himself—"I wonder where the heck he is"—and then explains to me why he's drinking herbal tea and not coffee.

"I wish I could have coffee. I could use the caffeine," he says, "but my band is playing a showcase tonight at Twelfth and Porter, and coffee does a number on my voice."

He squeezes his throat a couple of times as if he's making sure it's still there or identifying it in case I don't know where human vocal cords are located.

"Well, it's not the coffee that hurts them, but the *cream,* man— and I can't drink coffee without cream. My voice needs to be in top shape for this showcase."

Clearing his throat, he sips his tea.

"So I take it you're from out of town," I say.

Smiling, he nods. "Yeah. Lancaster, Pennsylvania."

"Oh, I've been there many times. My mother was infatuated with Amish people."

"We certainly have a lot of them," he says, like we're talking about white-tailed deer. "But they don't bother us too much, unless you get behind one of them on a busy street."

Before he can begin telling Amish jokes, I change the subject back to his show.

"By any chance," I say, qualifying my question first so that it doesn't offend him, "do you sing in a Christian band?" He looks surprised, so I add, "Too personal? Offensive? I promise I'm not going to try to evangelize you."

Adam laughs. "No, I'm not offended. I'm just surprised you asked me that. I never get that question back home. How did you know?"

"Just had a feeling," I say. "For some reason I'm pretty good at pointing out Christian rockers."

He laughs again and starts to blush. He seems to take my observation as a compliment. "What gave me away?"

"Eh, sometimes you can just tell."

"No, really, how did you know I was a Christian? It's obviously not the way I'm dressed. I don't dress like the everyday Christian. Is it a Holy Spirit thing?"

He's right; he doesn't dress like the ordinary Christian, but he does dress like the ordinary Christian rocker.

"I'm pretty sure it's not a Holy Spirit thing. It could be, I guess, but I think it's more like gaydar."

"What?" he says.

"It's different, of course, than assessing a person's sexual orientation, but not as much as you might think."

"Wow," Adam says. He's still smiling, but I'm not sure he means it as much as before. "That's…interesting."

I don't have the heart to tell him that he reeks of being a "Christian rocker." It didn't take a spiritual gift or a sixth sense to know what kind of music he made. My knowing the difference between a rocker and a Christian rocker is similar to the ability most people possess to distinguish a female from a drag queen. It's usually obvious, like the plot of a romantic comedy starring Matthew McConaughey.

No matter how elaborate the costume and makeup, drag queens can rarely fully disguise their masculine origins. Adam looks like a twenty-five-year-old purity pledge playing dress-up. He smiles too much—and too convincingly—to pull off a fashion statement rooted in the music and lifestyle of the Sex Pistols. I'm sure he's a nice guy and probably talented to some degree, but most of the punk rockers I know, even ones younger than Adam, look haggard, like they've lived several lifetimes. Or had to survive them.

"So what kind of music do you play? I mean, what style?"

"Most people say it's a mix of worship and pop punk." Adam looks at his watch again. "Us guys in the band call it *worshunk*." He smiles.

I laugh.

He starts laughing too, but I'm not sure we're laughing for the same reason. I'm laughing because it seems like the most obvious thing to do while I wait for him to retract his last statement with, "I'm just joking." He never does.

David arrives thirty minutes late. They shake hands and hug and tell me it's the first time they've met in person. Adam introduces David to me as Nashville's most awesome artist-development guy. David smiles, sits down, and the two of them begin talking about Adam's songwriting.

"I can't wait for you to hear the new song we've been working on," I hear Adam tell David at one point. "It's called 'Superstar Jesus.'"

"I can't wait," says David. "Great title, by the way."

I put my earbuds in and turn my iPod on shuffle. "Hide and Seek" by Imogen Heap begins playing, and the nausea I was beginning to feel subsides.

Music has always been present in my life, like God, fear, and McDonald's. I can't remember a day when music wasn't somehow involved. Music is like God in a lot of ways: Moving. Omnipresent. Unpredictable. And sometimes hard to get out of your head—even when you really want to.

I started spending the night with my grandmother and grandfather when I was four. Mammom loved music, but only the kind that played in churches or on PBS. God knew what I thought of PBS. From an entertainment standpoint, of the seven stations that my grandparents' antenna picked up, I ranked Maryland's public TV dead last.

As far as I was concerned, PBS fell off its rocker on weekends and every weekday morning after *The Electric Company*'s eight thirty time slot. If it wasn't between the hours of seven a.m. and nine a.m., when shows like *Sesame Street* and *Mister Rogers' Neighborhood* aired, PBS seemed pretty much useless unless you were old, crafty, or illiterate.

Mammom's obsession was *The Lawrence Welk Show,* a Technicolor variety hour featuring people who looked bred for perfection performing songs popular before Kennedy was shot.

Mammom's eyes were bad, so she'd sit on her knees about two feet away from the television. Lawrence was like an old friend to Mammom. She laughed at his corny jokes or blushed when he said something that would have been considered naughty in 1925. Sometimes she even talked to Lawrence as if he was singing in her living room.

"Oh Lawrence, you're so bad," she'd say, or if he was getting ready to announce the next song, she'd offer a suggestion. "Come on, Lawrence, I want to hear Buddy sing, or Norma." Then she'd look at me. "Actually, I like any of the singers except the Aldridge Sisters. They're too flashy. They think they're something special."

Mammom knew every song Lawrence's singers sang. Sometimes she sang along or tapped her hip with her hand or told me where she was or what she was doing the first time she heard it. Sometimes Lawrence played a song that made Mammom quiet, almost somber. If I spoke during those songs, she didn't respond. Sometimes she closed her eyes. Sometimes she cried. Sometimes she couldn't stop smiling. Music moved Mammom in ways I didn't understand; she didn't just listen, she felt it.

Years went by before I felt the freedom to feel music like that.

I was raised in an ultraconservative Baptist church where emotion and honesty were even less compatible than Christian fundamentalism and self-worth. At my church whenever somebody capable of emotional honesty became a member, it created a situation similar to my father's lectures about a new puppy: "As long as it never poops on the carpet, I'll let it be an 'inside dog.'" Anyone was welcome to join us for worship on Sundays, as long as they never emotionally pooped on the carpet. Most of us kids were "house-trained" before we'd memorized our multiplication tables.

Until I left for college at nineteen, I held most of my feelings in. Consequently, my early twenties weren't pretty. But they felt good.

That was when music became a companion.

Before MP3 players were invented, I was impressed when I could fit all my music in the backseat of my Oldsmobile Alero and still have enough room for two skinny friends or one fat one. I took my music collection with me everywhere. And for those occasions when I wasn't driving, I had a fifty-CD "therapy" binder where I kept my most important musical selections.

Some CDs I bought because of one popular song or for the band itself. When I purchased Garbage's first CD, *Garbage*, it wasn't because I thought Shirley Manson and crew rocked, necessarily, though on occasion "Only Happy When It Rains" made me feel good. The real reason was so I could tell my friends I *owned* Garbage's album. The same was true with P.M. Dawn's third album, *Jesus Wept*, and Marcy Playground's debut. In the nineties, owning the right CD equaled power: It could turn a longtime enemy into a best friend. It could make the cool crowd let you sit with them at church or at school.

A CD-induced spike in status was usually only temporary. In most cases the ego boost alone was worth the fifteen dollars or, if you were crazy enough to shop at Sam Goody, eighteen dollars. Once in a while the investment didn't pay off though, like Wilson Phillips's sophomore album, *Shadows and Light.* I thought for sure, based on the success of their debut, the purchase would help me in some way, but none of my friends cared, and in the end, it sort of hurt my reputation. Word got around that I listened to the whole thing in one sitting and liked three songs.

Most of the time, the music I bought was far more than just entertainment or status seeking.

In 1991 I bought Amy Grant's 1988 album, *Lead Me On.* I wasn't allowed to listen to Amy until I turned eighteen and was deemed by the government old enough to vote and fight in wars. That night I sat on my bed and listened to Amy sing stories for three hours. People at my church described Amy in a lot of different ways: Heathen. Satan's "angel." God's Madonna. One youth pastor told us that if Amy had been alive during biblical times, she would have been little more than a talented concubine. But that night in my bedroom, Amy's songs brought me some hope. I listened to *Lead Me On* over and over again until I memorized every lyric. The words she sang resonated with something deep inside of me that, at eighteen, I was only beginning to understand.

I had always valued music. Before I could talk, my mother claims I could sing. But *Lead Me On* was the first music to wake me up, to cause me to pay attention. The songs made me want to change. Sometimes when I listen to *Lead Me On,* the songs still make me want to change.

Good music changes me, shocks me, makes me feel uncomfortable, and drives me to think and hope and believe differently. And once in a while, it makes me cynical and sarcastic.

As Adam and David talk, I watch one of the spikes on Adam's head begin to wither. David watches it too but pretends it isn't happening. Eventually the spike's pointed tip falls over Adam's left eye. He pushes it out of the way, but it keeps falling.

Their conversation only becomes audible to me between songs. I hear David talk about his expectations for the band at tonight's showcase. I hear Adam discuss the band's desire to help end poverty. When I hear Adam say something about "connecting," I push Pause and listen.

"Our goal is to be real and honest when we're on stage," he says. "You know what I mean?"

David nods.

"'Cause if we're vulnerable, it's like we're giving our audience permission to become vulnerable too. In some ways the music, the look, the live show—it's all a means to an end, man. We want to usher people into the presence of God and see lives changed. I don't know if I'm doing a good job of explaining, but…"

Adam loses his thought and David nods. "You're making complete sense. That's exactly the kind of artist or band that we want on our roster: Vulnerable. Vulnerable is good."

I think about how many times I've heard this type of conversation. Hundreds, perhaps. The context is sometimes different, but much of the dialogue is the same—people talking about how to create something "real" and "authentic" rather than just being real and authentic. So many of us Christians are all about being *vulnerable,* especially when we're on stage, dressed up in a costume and wearing makeup, putting on a performance we consider "a means to an end."

There's a short lull in Adam and David's conversation. David pulls at the collar of his shirt and says, "Now, Adam, you're not planning on talking too much at the showcase, right?"

"I was planning on talking some; you know, so people get to know us."

David squints. "Hmm. I'd keep the talking to a minimum tonight. Most of the audience is going to be managers, booking agents, producers—those sorts of people. And they're not interested in hearing you talk, so let's keep the focus on the performance tonight."

It sounds like David has a bit of performance anxiety.

"Oh, okay. Whatever you say."

I take out my earbuds and begin packing up my belongings. Adam sees me preparing to leave.

"You heading out?"

"Yeah," I say, throwing my book bag over my shoulder. "Good meeting you and I wish you the best of luck tonight."

He smiles. "Thanks, I'll need it. Quick question. Check out the guy sitting in the corner." Adam shifts his eyes toward his right, indicating the tall man sitting alone with a cup of coffee and a book. "The guy dressed like a hobo, except his clothes look expensive. Is he a rocker or a Christian rocker?"

David laughs. "You're kidding, right?"

"No. Why?" Adam looks at the man more closely.

Shaking his head, David looks at me. "You tell him."

"That's Jack White," I say. "He's definitely not a Christian rocker."

Adam looks again. "Is he in a band?"

"Have you heard of the White Stripes?"

Adam's blank stare is familiar—full of innocence and wonder and curiosity. I know that expression. It wasn't long ago that I looked at people the same way.

"Can I get them on iTunes?" he asks.

"Yeah, you can," I say. "And you should buy the album. They're good. Give it a chance. It might teach you something about being vulnerable."

Gifted and Talented

God talked to me a lot when I was little. While playing in my sandbox or leaping over the garden sprinkler or serving the Lord's Supper to my father's bird dogs, I'd sometimes heard God calling my name.

He usually didn't have anything important to tell me. He just called to say hi and give me updates on what the angels were up to. The way he described it, heaven seemed pretty boring. Every time we talked, it seemed the angels were either singing songs of thanksgiving unto him, bowing down around his heavenly throne, or crying. Once in a while, during thunderstorms, God let them go bowling. But most of the time God just called to see if I was listening.

When I became old enough to read, God started making heaven sound more exciting. He used words like *luxurious* and *luminous* to describe the other side. Sometimes after talking to God, I'd tell my mother about our conversations. Mom was good at pretending she was interested in the things God and I talked about, but she was a Baptist through and through, which meant she approached her faith like the woman on the Bounty paper towel commercials: quick, with no time for nonsense like spiritual leaks and spills.

Once, I remember, I ran into the kitchen, picking up enough speed to make skidding to a stop difficult. "Guess what, Mom?" I said, breathing heavily, like somebody who'd just finished getting dunked in our church's baptismal pool. "When I get to heaven, God is going to give me my own planet."

Mom didn't say anything at first; she just turned in my direction and looked at me. Worry sat between her eyebrows.

"Honey." Mom smiled and wiped her hands on an old tea towel. "Are you sure God said he was going to give you a planet?"

"Yes, I'm sure," I said. "I remember because I've never been offered a planet before."

"I think you must have heard wrong, sweetie."

"No, I didn't hear wrong. God told me he would give me my own planet. Like Venus or Neptune. That's what I heard."

Unfortunately, not all the things God told me went along with our Baptist way of doing things. I learned quickly that what we believed as Baptists trumped anything God told me. The things he said didn't count unless they were included in my church's statement of faith.

"Aw, sweetie, we're Baptists." Mom's voice was serious, the same tone she used when she prayed for our friends with cancer or people who didn't like God. She didn't sound mean, just Christian. "Baptists don't get their own planets when they die and go to heaven. That's something the Mormons believe."

Mom yelled into the family room where my father sat in his orange recliner, watching a young Oprah Winfrey deliver the news on WJZ. "Virgil, is it Mormons who believe they get their own planet when they die?"

Dad muted Oprah and thought for a second. "Yeah, the Mormons believe that, but I think it's just the men who get a planet."

"See?" Mom took a deep breath. "I'm sure you just heard wrong, son."

"Or maybe I'm a Mormon."

"No," Mom and Dad barked in unison.

"You're a Baptist, Buck," Dad said, "and I don't want to hear any more about it."

I plopped down and rested my elbows on the kitchen table and my head in my hands. "Do Mormons believe in unicorns and big nectarines?"

"I don't think so," Mom said.

"Good. Because God also told me I could have a flying unicorn and all the basketball-sized nectarines I can eat."

God talked to me mostly about things like heaven, Jesus, and sin, and once in a while, he told me what my chickens were thinking about. He talked to a lot of other kids about their life's calling, as they called it, but I can't recall him ever telling me what he wanted me to be when I grew up. I wanted him to tell me, but only so I wouldn't feel out of place. Most of my friends claimed God told them their calling before they'd finished the third grade. He usually spoke to them during church services, after our pastor finished preaching his sermons.

Sometimes during the altar call, my friends walked up to the front of the church and whispered in Pastor Nolan's or a deacon's ear. That's what people did when God was busy doing official business with their hearts, minds, bodies, and souls.

I wasn't supposed to watch God do his business. Everyone in the congregation was supposed to close their eyes during an altar call.

Keeping your eyes open was considered sacrilegious and socially nosy. God's business was a spiritual matter. But I sometimes thought our church's altar should have come equipped with stalls, like the men's room.

It was difficult for me to close my eyes for long periods of time at that age. Partly because I got bored looking at the back of my eyelids, but mostly because I liked knowing which people in our church needed prayer and which ones didn't. Plus, when one of my friends walked forward to follow the Lord in believers' baptism, I liked looking for opportunities to wave at them.

At the end of the service, a pastor or deacon announced to the congregation the names of the people and what transaction they made with God. Usually the dealings regarded a person's eternal salvation or somebody deciding to follow Jesus in believer's baptism or join our church. But once in a while the announcement was about somebody hearing from God about his or her calling.

At some point in my childhood, nearly every one of my friends stood in front of the church and publicly professed that God had called them to be preachers or missionaries or choir directors, and if they were girls, that God had called them to be the wives of preachers, missionaries, or choir directors. As a church we got quite giddy any time God told somebody something about the future, but we became especially excited when God told a child what his or her career path should be.

After the service those kids got treated like famous people, the way heathens treated big-time celebrities like Bo, Luke, and Daisy from *The Dukes of Hazzard*. With their parents posing proudly by their sides, my friends stood in the front of the church while members of the congregation walked up and shook their hands, told them how proud we were that they decided to listen to God, and congratulated their parents on raising an obedient kid. At our church the experience was sort of like a bar mitzvah without the dancing, age restrictions, Scripture memorization, or party hats. Plus, because we were Baptists and not Jews, God was actually involved in our festivities. At least, that's what we believed.

It never happened to me. As much as I would have loved to hear God verbalize his perfect will for my life, it didn't happen—at least not with any divine clarity.

Instead of talking to me, God contacted other people about my calling when I was six years old, after I sang my first solo in my church's children's choir. My mom directed the kids' choir, and though she realized my keen vocal ability when I was four, she waited to showcase it because she wasn't sure I could handle the pressure of singing all by myself in front of a large crowd. But soon after my sixth birthday, Mom offered me the lead solo in the song "Pass It On (It Only Takes a Spark)."

I was excited about singing. The first thing I did was run next door and tell my best friend, Julie. Julie was thrilled for me, but she got a lot more excited after I sang the first line of my solo to her. "It only takes a spark to get a fire going."

A grin spread across Julie's face, and she clasped her hands together like she was about to get down on her knees and pray. "Will Smokey Bear be at your church when you sing?"

"I don't think so. Why would Smokey Bear come to our church?"

"Because of the song you're singing." Julie unclasped her hands and threw them up in the air. "It's about preventing forest fires, right?"

"Why would I sing about preventing forest fires at church?" I put my hands on my hips and looked at her like she was as crazy as Wednesday on *The Addams Family.*

Before Julie could answer my question, I explained that the song was about how Jesus liked starting fires in people's souls so they wouldn't burn in the flames of hell for eternity after they died. I stopped talking when Julie stared at me like *I* was the crazy one.

Later, my mom reminded me that Julie was Catholic and there-fore uncomfortable talking about God.

Soon after my debut, quite a few people at my church believed I was called to be a famous church singer. Their most notable indicator was my ability to sing like a girl. Possessing female vocal cords might not seem like a big deal, but at the church my family attended—Inde-pendent Baptist Bible Church (IBBC)—it was enough to convince a number of the members that I was spiritually gifted.

The folks who thought the Holy Spirit had dubbed me a vocal prodigy were the kind of people who thought that men who could hit the G above middle C without going off-key should be revered like kings or the Mandrell sisters. Their certainty about my gifting only strengthened as I got older. By the time I was eleven, they thought I might have my chance to star as the female voice in an all-male south-ern gospel quartet.

Even though I wasn't sure about God's call on my life, I was aware that I had a lot going for me. I was cute with a friendly demeanor, and capable of hitting high notes most girls only dreamed of reaching. Also, people told my parents all the time that I was the only kid in the children's choir talented enough to be on *Star Search.* As far as I was concerned, being hailed talented enough for *Star Search* by church members excited me a lot more than being dubbed gifted and talented by the Holy Spirit, mostly because if I won *Star Search,* I got a trophy I could enjoy here on earth.

The problem was that I wasn't allowed to watch *Star Search* because my mother thought the women who competed in the spokesmodel competition dressed like prostitutes. But I'd seen commercials, and once in a while, as I flipped through channels when my mother wasn't in the room, I watched the singers, dancers, and prostitutes perform until my stomach could no longer handle the anxiety of my mother possibly catching me.

I loved imagining myself on *Star Search.* When I was ten, I started having a recurring dream that I was standing on the *Star Search* stage, a spotlight shining in my face, waiting for Ed McMahon to announce that week's winner in the Junior Voice competition. I'd just brought the house down with a pitch-perfect rendition of Debby Boone's "You Light Up My Life," the only song I knew that couldn't be found in a hymnal.

Competing against me was a twelve-year-old, curly-headed blonde named Victory Gracen. A lot of people at church thought Victory was destined for Christian stardom, but I wasn't convinced. Victory could carry a tune, but only with her nostrils. Most of her performances sounded like head colds set to music, but her nasal congestion stayed on key, so people liked hearing her sing. Nevertheless, she never beat me when we competed on *Star Search;* my dream always ended with Ed announcing that the judges had given me four stars and Victory three and a quarter stars.

I knew my chances of performing on *Star Search* were slim. My family and I were country folk, the sort of people who felt awkward and fearful whenever we traveled to big cities without chaperones. The only influential connections my father had were with farmers or local politicians. Because of the people he knew, Dad could easily score a bushel of sweet corn or a prime hunting location; once in a while he could even get out of a traffic ticket. However, unless I wanted to sing at the Kent County 4-H Fair or twenty-five feet up a tree in a deer stand for an audience of opossums, Dad's contacts were useless.

I tried to push the *Star Search* dream out of my mind, but it was difficult when somebody at my church was always dreaming it on my behalf.

"Virgil Turner," Brother George called out one Sunday morning to my father. "You're just the man I wanted to see. I was thinking about your son yesterday afternoon."

"Why were you thinking about Matthew, George?"

"I was watching one of those entertainment shows on TV."

A farmer and usher at IBBC, Brother George was tall and quite skinny, except for a large belly that jutted over his belt, round and hard like a pregnant lady's. I couldn't understand how somebody could be frail from his chest up and also from his waist down, but suffer from obesity in the middle. It was fascinating.

I sometimes pictured Brother George sitting on his sofa in his living room with a bucket of fried chicken and a Shih Tzu perched atop his belly. One Sunday I realized the same thought had occurred to Brother George. As the pastor delivered his sermon, Brother George used his belly as a resting place for his Bible, reading glasses, and a box of Kleenex.

"Have you seen the singing competition?" Brother George stopped midsentence to lick his fingers and stroke his mustache. "It comes on in the afternoons on Saturdays." Smoothing out the hair on his upper lip, he thought for a moment. "Oh, what is that show's name? I know you've seen it, Virgil. The host is the old announcer from *The Tonight Show*, the '*Heeeerrrrreeeee's* Johnny' guy—Ed Mc-something."

The chances that my father knew Ed's last name were slim since he only watched TV shows that featured firearms or Charles Bronson. I tugged on Dad's pant leg.

"He's talking about Ed McMahon, the host of *Star Search*."

"Oh," said Dad, "I've never paid much attention to that show, George."

"You haven't watched *Star Search*?" Brother George tugged at his red suspenders. "Well, like I said, I was watching it yesterday, and when it got to the junior competition, it dawned on me that I knew a kid who could sing circles around either of those two amateurs." He smiled and nodded his head at me. "As you know, Virgil, Matthew sings like an angel—a *boy* angel, of course. But an angel nonetheless."

Brother George smiled proudly, as though he was the first to compare me to a heavenly creature. Actually, I got compared to angels all the time.

Once, when a woman shared with my mother that I sang like an angel, she added, "You'll think this is funny, Carole: while Matthew was singing, I leaned over to my husband and said, 'Ken, Carole and Virgil should have named that boy Lucifer.'"

"You think I should call him Lucifer? Just because he can sing?" Mom didn't get angry. She felt sorry for the lady. Stupid people always brought out Mom's compassionate side. Rather than acting shocked or infuriated, Mom stared at the woman with the same expression she gave small, furry mammals that she was contemplating petting. Mom's reaction caused the lady to backtrack.

"Oh Carole," she said, "I hope you don't think I was suggesting that Matthew was like the real devil. I said that because before Lucifer turned into Satan, he was the angel in charge of heaven's choir arrangements. So really, it's sort of a compliment being called Lucifer. Did you know Satan was once heaven's musical director? Look it up; it's in the book of Ezekiel. Some pastors think that's why Lucifer uses rock 'n' roll to help people find hell—because he was very musical. Like an evil Mozart."

On the way home from church, Mom told Dad and me about the conversation. "I think she's got a real problem, Virgil," Mom said. I saw Mom's point, but the more I thought about what the woman said, the more I began to realize how nice a compliment it really was. I didn't particularly like the name "Lucifer," but if I was going to possess one of Satan's many talents, his gift for music seemed like the safest bet. I knew people who had some of Satan's other talents, and often their gifts made them difficult people to be around, especially when they were on the deacon board.

I never wanted to believe that Lucifer had anything to do with my musical abilities, but considering my gift often caused me great temptation, it also seemed plausible.

Conversations like the one my father was having with Brother George always reminded me of that temptation: pride. As I listened to him tell Dad how he thought I was a shoo-in for *Star Search*, my head began to swell. Pride felt good, like the gentle tingling of my mother's fingernails massaging my head.

IBBC's pastor, Dave Nolan, a scholar of fundamentalism as well as a Bible trivia whiz, told us that finding pleasure in the accolades of man was sinful. When he put it like that, it sounded sinful, like it was something that only happened at rest stops on Interstate 95. Unlike the heathens who sought praise for their talents, Baptists were supposed to be humble about the things we were good at.

I envied the humility of some of the other talented folks at my church, like Florence Goodfox. A singer in our church, Ms. Florence performed "Onward Christian Soldiers" at every dead member's funeral and once a year at IBBC's Fourth of July Sunday celebration. Despite being a town celebrity—every bit as famous as Chestertown's mayor or the kid who played Arnold's brother on *Different Strokes*—on the occasions that I complimented Ms. Florence on her singing, she acted shocked and confused.

"Oh, that's not my talent up there on stage," she told me the first time. Then she pointed up at the ceiling. My eyes followed her finger. For a moment, both of us stood with our eyes directed upward toward the gold-plated chandeliers above our heads. "That's who you should be complimenting, Matthew, not me."

Not everybody cared for Ms. Florence. Even some of the most committed members swallowed her humility like it was cod-liver oil. But they didn't understand her like I did. I knew what it felt like to be both Baptist and talented, so Ms. Florence's modesty, though odd and difficult to believe sometimes, didn't leave me gagging behind her back.

One of my mother's friends, Miss Cheryl, was a God-fearing gossip. She and Mom sang in the choir together. I got the impression sometimes that Miss Cheryl was jealous of Ms. Florence's popularity. "I don't believe her humble act for one second," Miss Cheryl said to my mother one Wednesday evening. "Not wanting to be prideful is one thing, Carole, but telling people that your talent is actually God's talent isn't what I call humility."

"Is that what she thinks?" said Mom.

"Yes, Carole, that's what she thinks. That her talent is on loan from God."

Mom's mouth fell open like the drawer on a cash register. "I had no idea, Cheryl."

"And as you know, Florence makes mistakes once in a while. God doesn't make mistakes."

Miss Cheryl had a point, but she also didn't have much of a reason to be humble about her singing ability.

At some point in the conversation, Brother George reminded my father of the time I sang the lead vocal in "Sweeter Gets the Journey," a favorite at IBBC. "Remember when Matthew sang the part that goes…" Brother George cleared his throat and started what he called singing, "Up to that heavenly shore, we'll live forever more. Never have a worry; never have a care. Everything will just be happiness there…"

"Yeah, I know the song, George."

"But do you remember that part of the song? The part that—"

Before Brother George could start again, my father interrupted, "Yes, I remember that part. My wife directs the children's choir, so I've heard it quite a few times."

"Oh, that's right," said Brother George. "Then maybe you understand how difficult a part that is to sing and remain on pitch. I can't do it. But Matthew can, Virgil. He sang it flawlessly. That's incredible for a kid his age."

"You think so?" said Dad.

"Matthew's voice has brought tears to my eyes. That hasn't happened since the first time I heard Karen Carpenter." Brother George looked at me. "You have a tremendous talent, young man. You know that, right?" He smiled and raised his eyebrows in anticipation of my response.

Just as I was about to point at the ceiling to offer credit where credit was due, I opened my mouth and said, "Yes sir, I know I can sing pretty good. And I've had dreams about being on *Star Search*. I'd love to go on that show. I've been practicing a new song at home during my free time…"

I stopped midsentence when I felt the firm grip of my father's left hand on my shoulder—his nonchalant way of telling me I was embarrassing him. Dad enjoyed my singing, but he didn't want Brother George to know that I practiced my stage performance in front of a full-length mirror in my bedroom, using one of Dad's screwdrivers as my microphone. Girls use hairbrushes. Boys use screwdrivers. That was my rule.

"Well, anyway, Virgil," said Brother George, "Matthew sings better than any eleven-year-old I know. And I think he'd be a perfect candidate for *Star Search*. In my opinion, he'd be a shoo-in to make the semifinals. He's got talent and he's a good-looking kid."

Brother George talked like someone with connections to the entertainment world. I figured he might know a talent scout or a deejay or a friend of a friend of a cousin who knows a cameraman who lives in Los Angeles. I was impressed.

"And, Virgil, think about what kind of witness for Jesus Matthew could be with exposure like that. I can just see it. Jesus wins *Star Search*. Wouldn't that be great?"

"It really would, George." My father looked at me and I knew exactly what he was thinking: *I wish this man would shut up.* "I wish we knew how to get Matthew on a show like that."

"Well, that's why I wanted to talk to you. I've got an idea. Now, it's not *Star Search,* but it would be a good place to start."

Brother George explained that a church in south Delaware was having a music competition for Baptists. "I'm helping the youth pastor spark up some qualified candidates. Do you think Matthew might want to compete in the solo division?"

I did want to go—far more than I was allowed to display in front of people who had never seen me in my underwear. I remained visibly unmoved on the outside, but on the inside I was already thinking about what song I would sing and whether I would hold the microphone during my performance or keep it on the stand. So many decisions.

Three months later I stood on a church stage in Seaford, Delaware, at the annual youth convention for the Eastern Shore Association of Independent Fundamental Baptist Churches.

Fifteen hundred strangers sat in pews, gawking at me as I grabbed the microphone and slipped it off the stand. I sang an old gospel song by Andrae Crouch called "Through It All." I sang it a cappella because the pianist at the convention only played by ear and didn't know the song.

As I sang, I thought, *Brother George was right; this isn't anything like* Star Search. *No special lights. No cameras. No Ed McMahon. No prostitutes.* The only part of the experience that resembled my dream was my performance. When I sang my last note, the audience's applause erupted. Half of them stood up and clapped.

Later that evening, after a sermon, an altar call, and the presentation of boys and girls who had decided God wanted them to be pastors, missionaries, choir directors, or their wives, a tall man in a plain suit walked up to the podium and, with about as much excitement as a robot reading a passage out of Leviticus, leaned into the microphone and said, "I'm going to announce the winners for this year's singing competition."

The solo vocalist category was the last to be announced. My circulatory system felt like it was overheating as I waited for Mr. No Personality to read the name of the winner.

"The winner of this year's solo competition is…" He paused for a moment to clear his throat and then said, "Matthew Turner."

People hooted and hollered as I walked up to receive a thirteen-inch-tall blue and gold trophy. As Mr. No Personality handed it to me, the two of us smiled for the convention's photographer, and I nervously walked back to my seat.

I felt more alive than I had ever felt before. It didn't matter that only three other performers sang in the competition, one of them a kindhearted deaf kid who had definitely not heard himself sing. Still, it felt good to win. There's nothing like hearing for a few moments the love and acceptance of fifteen hundred people. I savored every last clap. I let the pride flush my face and I didn't feel ashamed.

For two and a half minutes, until I heard the final clap, I felt called.

Fanatic

Each summer Dad started talking about the Gideons' picnic a month in advance, making sure it was on our calendars so we could plan to attend. As soon as Dad brought up the Gideons' picnic each year, my teenage sisters, Melanie and Kelley, began making plans to be busy that day.

"You're not going to the picnic?" Dad was always the last to know. "Aw, hon, why not?"

"Because they're all old people, Dad," Melanie or Kelley said. Mom and Dad were the youngest Gideons in our county. "It's like a geriatric picnic, and that's not fun."

My father loved showing off his family at picnics. Work picnics. Family reunions. Picnics for senior citizens who helped smuggle Bibles into foreign countries. Dad was proud of his family because he was convinced he had the most beautiful family in Kent County. My mother, sisters, and I pretended to be modest about Dad's gushing, but really, we thought he was right. Kent County wasn't known for being home to the most beautiful people in the world, so agreeing with Dad wasn't haughtiness. It was just true: comparatively, we were a good-looking family.

Sometimes, in order to have his beautiful family all in one place, Dad tried to sweeten the deal.

"Well, some of those old people are going to have crabs," my father coaxed, almost singing the word *crabs*. "You don't get to have crabs very often."

Picnicking with old people who have crabs might have been a turnoff most of the time, especially for teenage girls, but that wasn't true for those who grew up on the Eastern Shore of Maryland. Most of us would do just about anything for crabs. For my sisters, crabs made the picnic much more difficult to resist. Well, at least for Melanie. Eleven years older than me, my oldest sister loved crabs more than any human being I knew, so Dad usually talked her into attending. But the bribe rarely worked on Kelley. She liked crabs, but not enough to spend six and a half hours picnicking with the oldest Christians in Kent County.

Each summer I worried more about the future of the Gideons, because most of them seemed to be on their deathbeds. Nearly all of them carried some kind of inanimate support system: canes, walkers, respirators, or devices that beeped if their hearts stopped or if they stood too close to a police scanner. I always wished the picnic was adjacent to a hospital, or at the very least, within shouting distance of a medevac unit. It was stressful, wondering if one of them would die while eating potato salad.

Talking to old people was exhausting, for me anyway, especially the ones I didn't see regularly. I hated talking to the old ladies the most. They weren't mean or anything, just slow and boring like the Hardy Boys mysteries when I actually had to *read* them instead of watch them on TV. And most of the old ladies smelled like spiked pond water.

I went through the same routine every summer. As soon as I arrived at the picnic, a clan of old ladies saw me and looked me up and down like a pack of hyenas circling a baby antelope. Then one of them usually said, "Oh, goodness me, you're Virgil Turner's son, aren't you? You are the spitting image of your daddy."

"Yes ma'am," I said in my friendly tone. They might have been slow, boring, and scented like fermented algae, but I was always respectful for fear that my father would rub my nose into one of them. But it did get tiring. It required my undivided attention, perfect eye contact, and a grin or full-on smile to prove my parents were raising me properly.

"Boy, you are getting tall," one of the old ladies said, and then she laughed and nudged one of the deaf or blind ladies sitting next to her. "Ain't Matthew getting tall? Can you believe that's Virgil's boy? Matthew, how old are you now? Eight? Nine?"

I sighed. "I'll be thirteen in November."

"Thirteen? You're *thirteen*? I guess you haven't gotten as tall as I thought."

And then one of the nearly deaf ladies added, "He's like that kid who played Webster on the television. Wasn't it sad how puny that boy was? He was a cute kid, though."

I always managed to force a smile, but I hated being a late bloomer, because sometimes I couldn't help worrying that I might actually have the same disease as Gary Coleman. Especially when confronted with the possibility by every old lady in Kent County.

The summer before I turned fourteen, Kent County's Gideons moved their August gathering to the home of their newest members, nonelderly people like Mom and Dad.

On the drive to the Smythes' house, Mom turned to look at

Elisabeth and me in the backseat. "Now, kids, the Smythes are very nice people, but they go to the Church of God. Don't act strange if you hear them talk funny."

"The church of *God*?" Elisabeth rolled her eyes at me. "That's a weird name for a church. I thought we went to God's church."

"We do go to God's church," I assured her, then tapped Mom's arm. "What do you mean when you say the Smythes talk funny? Like the Japanese lady who comes to church?"

"No," Mom said, "not like that. Some of their religious expressions are peculiar, like how they articulate God stuff. It's just obvious they're not Baptists, that's all."

Mom wasn't being unkind, just born-again Baptist. It was completely natural for us to relate to another person's brand of Christianity by comparing it, critiquing it, and pointing out how it was inferior to our own. It never crossed our minds that such an act was judgmental; in fact, most of us thought pointing out the flaws of other denominations was a true sign of faithfulness.

Eyes bulging, Dad looked at Mom. "What are you talking about, hon? I've never heard the Smythes talk funny. They're very nice people."

"I said they were nice people." Mom took off her sunglasses and pulled the visor down so she could look at her face in the mirror. "But they do talk funny, and you know it."

Looking in the mirror, Mom stretched the skin beneath her eyes and made what few lines she had disappear. Holding the mirror, she inspected her face from various angles. Mom was always concerned about looking old. No matter how many times people told her she looked ten years younger than her age, sometimes she needed to see it or imagine it for herself.

"I've talked to Mr. Smythe many times," Dad said. "I don't think there's an odd thing about him."

"Maybe he isn't weird, Virgil. I haven't talked to him all that much. I do think he has the largest head I've ever seen, and it's shaped like Mr. Potato Head. But I've spent plenty of time chatting and praying with Mrs. Smythe—and *she* talks funny."

Dad shook his head. "I've had conversations with her, Carole, and she's never said one thing out of the ordinary about God to me."

Mom grinned into the mirror and checked her teeth. "Well, trust me, Virgil, I've heard her say some very out-of-the-ordinary things about God." Mom looked at me through the mirror. "Just so you know, your father is wrong. The woman is a bit cuckoo. I'm not saying she'll say anything strange today, but she has. That's all."

"What funny things have you heard her say?" Dad asked.

"I can't remember exactly. Just some things she said about God." Mom scraped a fingernail against one of her front teeth. "She makes it pretty obvious she's *not* Baptist. You know how you can sometimes tell. She uses flashy words. Flamboyant, even. She's different. But she's very nice."

A few minutes later Dad parked the car on the street in front of the Smythes' house. I climbed out of the backseat and prepared myself to meet Mrs. Smythe. I thought I knew what to expect. Mom and I shared a common gift for reading people, as well as an inability to put our character examinations into words. But we knew what the other meant. In my mind I pictured Mrs. Smythe as a Christian clown, or like God's version of a female Pee-wee Herman.

The four of us walked to the front door. Dad knocked and then walked inside.

"Hello, Turner family!" Mrs. Smythe did something that resembled a hop as she came toward us. It wasn't a skip, but it was definitely not a walk either. Later, when Mom and I talked about it, we decided to call it a prancing curtsy. "It's very British looking," Mom said.

Mrs. Smythe hugged Mom like she was an old high school friend.

"Oh Carole." She hopped in place and then held Mom's arms with her hands. "I'm so happy you're here. It's such a wonderful blessing from our Abba God to have you and your lovely family in our home." She glanced at Elisabeth and me. As she stared at us, her thin lips slowly morphed into a huge smile. Her mouth looked like a blossom opening to display beauty and cheer to everyone lucky enough to notice it.

"We're happy to be here," Mom said, smiling.

"Isn't the weather just lovely?"

"Oh yes, the weather is amazing."

Mrs. Smythe's eyeballs danced as she and Mom shared a moment of Christian love and smiled at one another.

I stood there expecting cartoon bluebirds, mice, and squirrels to come inside and help us sew a quilt or bake pies.

Then Mrs. Smythe walked over to the bay window in her living room and looked longingly at the flower bed outside. Staring out the window, she spoke to her begonias.

"As soon as the sun shone through the blinds in our bedroom this morning, I leapt out of bed, opened the shades, and said aloud, 'This is the day that you, O God, have made, and I will celebrate and be happy in it!'"

I was shocked, partly because Mrs. Smythe was acting as though she stood on a stage performing *Macbeth,* but also because she quoted

Scripture from a false version of the Bible. Probably the *Living Translation,* I thought.

"And then I went out on the porch." Mrs. Smythe turned slowly toward us. "I needed to bask in the presence of the Lord. It's so inspiring to do that on occasion. It felt like Easter morning. Do you know what I mean, Carole?"

"Oh sure, I know exactly what you mean. I love to bask." Mom's eyes flicked sideways toward Dad. "Isn't that right, Virgil? Don't I love to bask?"

Dad nodded but without his usual smile. He'd seen enough drama for one day. That, or he felt embarrassed that Mom was right about Mrs. Smythe: she did talk funny.

Despite her curious God-talk, there was something charming about Mrs. Smythe's quirkiness. The way she moved. Her expressive eyebrows. Her sentence structure, so unique and outlandish. At some point during her performance, I realized she reminded me of Jim and Tammy Faye Bakker from the *Praise the Lord* television show.

My father loathed Jim and Tammy's television show. He insisted that good Baptists shouldn't watch shows that made God seem like a combination banker, therapist, and Mary Kay makeup consultant. But Jim and Tammy intrigued my untarnished imagination. When Dad wasn't home, I flipped back and forth between watching *The Flintstones* and Jim and Tammy's *PTL.*

Dad walked into the family room once and caught me with my eyes glued on Jim and Tammy performing one of their prayers.

"Buck, what else is on?" He plopped down in his recliner. "Sports. News. *Anything* but this."

"But, Dad," I screeched, "I have to see how this ends. Miss

Tammy's getting ready to pray for a woman in Kansas whose forearm is paralyzed because she tripped over her cat and fell down the stairs. Please let me see what happens."

I loved watching Tammy pray. When she talked to God, she put her whole body into the routine, like a gymnast on the uneven bars. My favorite part was when Tammy sobbed out to God. She sobbed with beauty and grace and utter hysteria, but I loved her.

Glaring at me, his hands on his sides, Dad said, "These people are crooks, Buck. They're always asking for money."

I didn't even look up. Dad was a doubter. He didn't believe in the power of twenty-four dollars a month like I did. When Tammy began praying for the poor Kansas woman with the numb forearm, both of us fixed our eyes upon her glorious ability to work it before God.

Once in a while I felt guilty about my fascination with *PTL*. It was so different from how we did things at our church. Maybe that explained why I had a hard time turning away when it came on. The set of *Praise the Lord* looked rich and golden. My church had gold-colored carpet, but it was old and dirty, and some of our pews had holes in the padding. I wondered why my church couldn't look like King Nebuchadnezzar's palace with a plush and luxurious stage that included a couple of half-naked sculptures of biblical characters sitting next to large, fake palm trees. I thought Pastor Nolan would look fantastic with a faux skyline of Jerusalem set up behind him while he preached.

Tammy Faye finished praying, wiped away her tears, and then sang a special song just for Ms. Kansas. *Wow,* I thought, *I wish she'd sing a special song for me.*

I looked at Dad. "Do you think Jim and Tammy Faye are angels?"

Dad's blank stare morphed into a scowl. "Would you just turn to channel 13? The news is on."

Mrs. Smythe acted angelic—like Tammy Faye without the fake eyelashes.

An hour later my family, the Smythe family, and about twenty senior citizens sat down for a potluck dinner and crabs. Mrs. Smythe sat down last. She placed a hot plate of tuna casserole on the table, then turned on some music.

Great, I thought. *Temptation.*

I didn't know any other Church of God people, but I assumed, because they weren't like Baptists, that they probably liked rock 'n' roll. I was half right.

Percussion laced the background music Mrs. Smythe played. Independent Fundamental Baptists hated drums, tambourines, and cymbals because the devil loved them and used them in all the music he sold at record stores.

As one of the old men taught me his "secret" way of opening a crab, I tried really hard not to listen to the female Satan singing in the background. The more I tried to shut out the music, the more I listened. This sinful music seemed different. The drums and the tambourines didn't overpower the singer's voice, and most shocking, the woman sang about God.

Mom noticed it too.

"June, who is this delightful singer?" she asked Mrs. Smythe, shaking her head in amazement.

"That's Sandi Patty," shouted Mrs. Smythe from the kitchen. "She's inspired, Carole. I believe with all my heart that her voice is chock full of the Holy Spirit. You couldn't get any more Holy Spirit in that voice if you wanted to."

"I haven't heard of her."

"Oh, that's a tragedy! You should borrow one of our cassette tapes. Her voice is anointed. Oh, you have to hear this…"

Mrs. Smythe walked over to her stereo, fumbled through her music collection, and changed the cassette. Mom yelled for Elisabeth and me to come and listen.

"Carole, this right here is Sandi's rendition of 'The Star-Spangled Banner.' It's the best I've ever heard."

By the time Sandi Patty had sung "at the twilight's last gleaming," Mom and I were shaking our heads at one another. "She's good, huh?" said Mom.

I nodded. Sandi's music was like nothing I had ever heard before. Christian. Worldly. Inspirational. Seductive. Listening to her sing made me feel tingly all over. I'd never experienced that feeling before—at least not from music.

That was a life-changing day for me. Sandi's talent was one of a kind in my opinion. Her voice leaped tall buildings in a single note. Because of the vocal acrobatics she performed while singing the national anthem, I became a megafan of Sandi Patty, and therefore withdrew my application of ever being considered "cool" in high school.

But I soon discovered that being a fan of Sandi would not be easy and that my devotion to her would eventually lead to all sorts of persecution.

In the 1980s Sandi was one of three multiplatinum-selling Christian music artists. The other two were Amy Grant and Petra. Just like the artists who sang about their love of sex, money, drugs, or Satan, Sandi sold out huge concert arenas, had a fan club, and even her very own tour bus. Her live shows featured ten-piece bands, full orchestration, and background singers.

Sandi's style of music is difficult to describe, because she's in a class all her own. Her songs combined gospel, Broadway, pop, jazz, blues, and opera. And oddly, it worked. At least to me it did. For a kid not allowed to listen to music that contained percussion of any kind, Sandi became my Madonna, Debbie Gibson, Barbra Streisand, Karen Carpenter, and Aretha Franklin all rolled into one.

But my church hated Sandi. They claimed the devil used her to lead people toward hell. Mom and I thought that was hogwash. We couldn't see how anybody would find hell via Sandi.

I found comfort in that. Since many in my church deemed her evil, being Sandi's fan made me feel edgy and full of rage, like I was bucking the fundamentalist system. I didn't get many opportunities to buck. I rarely felt the need to. But Sandi's music was contraband at IBBC. Not "cool" contraband like candy cigarettes or owning the first season of *V* on VHS. Nobody garnered popularity points getting caught with a Sandi Patty cassette in their pocket. That was like a guy admitting he sort of liked the song "Karma Chameleon" by Culture Club or piercing the wrong earlobe to make a statement. If a teacher learned about my loyalty to Sandi, they labeled me a heathen; if one of the kids at my Christian school found out, they assumed I was gay.

I felt sorry for Sandi. If merely being a fan was stressful and overwhelming, I couldn't imagine what it was like to be her. People said all sorts of cruel things about Sandi. They made fun of her music. They said her voice was shrill and unbearable. They called her names like

Sandi Fatty or Sandi Cow Patty. Sometimes I wondered how she continued to sing with such a glowing smile.

But the meanspiritedness of people didn't deter my devotion to Sandi one bit. Remaining faithful to her wasn't easy, but her music became my escape; it created a haven where I could be myself and see God as bigger than others believed he was.

I needed Sandi, and I suspected she needed me too.

Fifteen months after being introduced to Sandi, I overheard a conversation about her between two of my teachers in the school cafeteria. My ears perked up when I heard her name mentioned. I didn't know if their conversation was kind or hateful. Both were conservative, rule-following Baptists, so I had a feeling they hated her. But why were they whispering? Public discussions about Sandi weren't frowned upon unless they were positive. Anti-Sandi comments were welcomed and verbalized frequently at church and school. Even the little old ladies who volunteered their time to make lunches at school spewed hatred about Sandi.

On her 1986 album, *Morning Like This,* Sandi included a song called "Love in Any Language." The song began with Sandi singing "I love you" in five different languages, and then going on to sing about humanity's need for love. Critics of Sandi loved that song, not because of its message, but for its ammunition value. They used the song against her for two reasons: (1) because the lyrics didn't mention Jesus or God, and (2) many believed the song was a complete lie. They claimed that "I love you" in Arabic did not mean the same as it did in American.

One of the lunch ladies was up in arms about it.

"Do you know they played that song on WRBS this morning?" Mrs. McDoring flopped a handful of french fries into a carton and looked around to see who was listening. I stood at the counter, waiting for my pizza to come out of the oven. A couple of the other volunteers signaled to Mrs. McDoring that they were listening.

"I couldn't believe that a *Christian* radio station would broadcast such filth." She poured a bag of frozen fries into a metal basket and dropped them into the hot grease. "So you know what I did? I called them up and asked why they were playing New Age music on a station that is supposed to be glorifying our Lord and Savior. And I told them if I heard that song one more time, I would no longer support their ministry with these ears."

"Good for you, Lucille," said one woman.

Another nodded her head. "What did they say?"

"Oh, I had to leave a message with the receptionist. But I told the girl to write down that I was fuming mad about this, and that I was very serious about never listening again if they played her. She told me she would."

"Good for you for standing up for God," a lady said.

"You gotta get angry once in a while, you know?" Mrs. McDoring opened the oven, pulled out my pizza, and tossed it on a paper plate. Plopping it down in front of me, she said, "There you go, sweetie. Thanks for being so patient. Have a blessed afternoon."

Mrs. McDoring's feelings were pretty standard for the school faculty, so I figured the teachers whispering about Sandi must hate her too. Before I got the chance to find out if they were really anti-Sandi, they stopped talking. A couple of weeks went by before I learned the truth.

I ran into one of them at Pizza Hut. My father had sent me inside to pick up our takeout order. As soon as I walked in, I noticed Mr. Hanson and his family.

Seeing people from church in places other than church excited me. It was similar to going bird-watching on a nature trail, and then, among all the sparrows, crows, robins, wrens, and starlings that blended into nature's background, sighting an emu.

"Hello, Mr. Hanson," I said, waving at him from across the restaurant.

He acknowledged my greeting with a nod. "Mr. Turner."

That's how Mr. Hanson greeted everybody who was male: bobbing his head and reciting their last names. Most people thought he was being uppity, but not me. I assumed he acted that way because of his personality disorder, the one that made him a fantastic middle school teacher but quite difficult to get to know.

As he walked in my direction, I racked my brain for a way to bring up the topic of Sandi Patty. Discussing musical contraband off school and church property would be less stressful.

I could just ask him if he likes her, I thought, but quickly decided against that, because if he hated her, he might cause a scene. That's when I got the idea to softly sing "Let There Be Praise," one of my favorite Sandi songs.

I started half-mumbling, half-singing Sandi's inspirational tune. I crossed my arms and held my body tight, looking around the room as though I didn't know I was singing. Mr. Hanson arrived at the cash register to pay for his meal, but instead of pulling out his wallet, my singing caused him to look at me curiously. Now that I had his attention, I just kept singing. Stuck my hands in my pocket. Pulled them out. Checked my watch. Looked at the ads for lost children on the back of the papered menus.

"Matthew, are you singing?"

"Oh, was I?"

"I think you were. I thought I heard you singing."

My face turned red. "I might have been. Sometimes I sing without even knowing I'm doing it."

Mr. Hanson seemed to hesitate for a moment. Finally, he said, "Matthew, were you singing a Sandi Patty song?"

I put my head down and nodded.

"Oh, don't be ashamed." He grabbed my shoulder and whispered, "My family and I are fans of her too."

I breathed a fake sigh of relief. "You are?"

"Yes," he said, "and you'll be happy to know we're not alone. There are others like us at church."

"People who like Sandi? Mr. Hanson, that's amazing. I love Sandi so much. It feels so good to admit that out loud."

"I know, doesn't it? Freedom is an amazing thing, huh?"

"It really is."

I wanted to hug Mr. Hanson. It just felt so good to be able to talk to somebody other than my mother about my affection for all things Sandi. For ten minutes he and I discussed our favorite songs, which albums we liked best, and how we really wanted to see her live.

"You know she's coming to the Patriot Center in Virginia, right?" Mr. Hanson gazed around Pizza Hut to make sure nobody was listening. "There's a small group of us going if you and your family would like to attend."

A couple of months later, the covert operation "See Sandi Sing" was set in motion. Weeks prior to her Make His Praise Glorious concert, tickets had been bought, carpooling assignments handed out, and a meeting place set. On the afternoon of the concert, sixteen of us met in the Acme parking lot, piled into two minivans and a sedan, and drove almost three hours to northern Virginia.

Sandi's performance was two and a half hours of heaven, and not simply because her performance was brilliant and entertaining. At some point during the concert, it became more than that.

During one of her songs, I took my eyes off the stage and looked at the people sitting close to me. I couldn't remember a time when I had been among so many different kinds of Christians. White people. Black people. Baptists. Catholics. Amish. Pentecostals. The black man sitting next to me kept closing his eyes and raising his hands. A few times I saw him mumble words under his breath. A priest sitting several rows in front of me never moved the entire night. He didn't clap or stand up. I'm not even sure he knew who Sandi was. But I did see him smile a couple of times. A fat lady in tight sweatpants danced in the aisle. Most of us wouldn't have felt comfortable worshiping together on Sunday morning, but that didn't seem to matter. The music was powerful enough to not only make us forget that we were different—for two and a half hours, those differences didn't matter.

Clapping and singing, Elisabeth leaned over and whispered in my ear, "I think this is what heaven is going to be like."

You Gotta
Have Faith

All the well-behaved young men in my church, at least those my mother wanted me to be like, played the piano. Many of them demonstrated their talent during church services while the ushers passed around the offering plate. They wore suits and thick-rimmed glasses and were always polite to adults. When they sat at a piano, their fingers became fine-tuned machines capable of bringing the notes printed on sheet music alive. When I sat at a piano, my fingers became like ten chipmunks scampering across the keys, distracted and incapable of being trained.

The other young men played arrangements by Mozart and Bach and Handel. I played "Heart and Soul" with the precision of a sumo wrestler in a tutu.

I wanted to be a great pianist worthy of showcasing my ability during the church offertory, but I lacked natural talent—the talent of practicing. This never stopped me from taking piano lessons. I studied piano, off and on, for eight years, but I only practiced between lessons, off and on, for about a quarter of that time. Most of my practicing fell during my sophomore year, when Ms. Lansing was my instructor.

An eccentric Baptist, one who occasionally swore by the healing powers of a small glass of zinfandel, Ms. Lansing didn't belong in our church. She was a misfit, like Rudolph, the Red-Nosed Reindeer, with someone always calling her a name behind her back. Most often they called her an odd duck. The word *hen* or *bird* might also be employed, or they might refer to her as a "loose cannon." The people of our church thought she was as loony as a Democrat.

Ms. Lansing lived alone in an old two-story Victorian home in downtown Chestertown. Nobody knew how old she was, just that she was unmarried and cynical about it.

"Matthew," she said to me more frequently than I liked, "I need to find myself a man. Do you know any charming single or divorced men?" Then she laughed and waved a hand and added, "Oh, I'm just kidding. I don't really need a man."

I never knew what to say when she talked about being lonely so casually. That sort of conversation felt out of place at a forty-five-minute piano lesson. Most of the time I just chuckled, but only at the appropriate moments. If I'd been older, I might have offered some advice. In my mind, I told her, "You know what your problem is, Miss Lansing? You're like oatmeal in a world of Pop-Tarts. People like Pop-Tarts. Put some perfume on. You don't stink, exactly, but you smell like a librarian, boring and dusty. Everybody knows you're an excellent piano player, and I think you're an engaging conversationalist. But Ms. Lansing, you dress like a Quaker."

At this point, I imagined switching to a more compassionate tone. "Listen. Some people like oatmeal. My dad loves it. My grandmother eats it three or four times a week, because it's healthy, nourishing, and keeps her regular. But without butter and brown sugar, oatmeal tastes like Styrofoam. And I think that's how a lot of men see you, Ms. Lansing, like a plain sheet of Stryrofoam. Useful, but not interesting."

My mother would have killed me if I ever shared any of this advice out loud, so when Ms. Lansing talked about wanting to be married, I just nodded and told her I would pray that God would put a man in her life. If she found a good Baptist husband, her life would be easier because the women at church would like her more. She often told me about a deacon's wife who stared at her with mournful eyes.

"I think some women at IBBC feel sorry for me," she said, "as if they think I'm only half the woman I could be because I don't have a husband to act as my spiritual leader. And I suppose they think it's impossible for me to be happy because I don't know the joys of submissive behavior."

But that was only one reason people thought Ms. Lansing was strange. Others considered her rebellious because she was the only churchgoer who lived on Water Street. One of the oldest streets in downtown Chestertown, Water Street was largely populated with rich, influential heathens—politicians, lawyers, and college professors who trusted in the U.S. Constitution more than they trusted God. Certain people didn't understand why a Baptist, especially an unmarried female one, would want to live on such a Godforsaken avenue.

Ms. Lansing's independent spirit made her endearing. Sure, this same spirit convinced her to avoid the social pressures of purchasing a curling iron, but it also made her brave and, to some degree, unafraid. A different kind of Baptist than what I was used to, Ms. Lansing didn't seem to care about what other people thought about her odd ideas and peculiar way of doing things. Anybody who lived without the fear of hurting people's feelings had much more faith than the average Baptist. She certainly had more faith than me.

One afternoon, right in the middle of my playing the hymn "Work, for the Night Is Coming," Ms. Lansing patted me on the back. I stopped playing and looked at her.

"Choppy," she said, standing up and shooing me off the piano bench. When she sat down, she glared over her shoulder at me as though my playing offended her. "I'm sorry to stop you in the middle of your song, but I had to. I was beginning to feel a bit premenstrual."

I had no idea what "premenstrual" meant, but if the expression on her face was any indication, it wasn't Christlike.

I watched Ms. Lansing move the hymnal a few inches to her left and glance down at her feet to make sure they were close to the pedals. She looked at me again. "Hymns are tricky animals, Matthew. You can't do too much messing around with their melody and structure." She smirked. "A lot of times, the only thing a hymn has going for it is the purity of its melody. I have no idea what you were doing to this poor hymn, but I was ready to reach inside my purse and find my razor blades."

She smirked again. "That was a joke. But I do carry razor blades in my purse. They're handy for cleaning bug guts off the windshield."

She put her hands in middle-C position. "Now listen to how I play this." A few bars into the hymn, she asked, "Do you hear the difference?"

I listened to her play for a moment.

"I hear the difference," I said, "but now it sounds like something Enya would do."

"Enya? You think so?"

Ms. Lansing appeared to like being compared to somebody outrageous like Enya, which didn't surprise me, because she didn't mind telling people that sometimes she prayed with her eyes open. But Enya offended me.

I'd only heard one of Enya's songs. My cousin Jay played it for me when my family visited his in Montana a few months before. The song sounded spooky, seductive, and made me feel sensations I knew didn't come from the Holy Spirit.

Still playing, Ms. Lansing asked, "Is sounding like Enya a bad thing?"

"I think it is," I said. "Her music is New Age."

"Who told you that?"

"It's pretty obvious."

"And what makes it obvious, Matthew? I want to know."

I sighed. Ms. Lansing knew very well why Enya's music was New Age. For starters, it was always shelved in the New Age section at Sam Goody. But mostly, and this was what made Enya's songs so dangerous: "Because it's pennywhistle music."

Ms. Lansing banged a minor chord.

"It's true," I said. "Native Americans like pennywhistle music. And you know those people who wear the funny-looking hats and charm snakes? They like it too."

She spun around on the piano bench and looked at me the same way Mrs. Garrett on *The Facts of Life* looked at Tootie at least three times an episode—like I'd been born adorable but without a brain.

"People who wear silly hats and charm snakes, Matthew?" she said. "Do you mean Pentecostals?"

"I don't think so." I tried to remember if I'd ever encountered a Pentecostal wearing a hat that resembled a beehive. I'd seen a bunch of female Pentecostals with hairdos that looked like beehives, and a couple of those women claimed Jesus gave them the power to handle venomous snakes, but pennywhistles weren't involved.

Ms. Lansing closed her eyes and began taking slow, deep breaths, one right after another in perfect rhythm. I hadn't realized how odd it was to watch somebody breathe. Intentional breathing seemed like one of those things people did in private unless they were Jane Fonda or hooked up to a respirator. A few moments later, she spoke.

"Just give me a second to calm down, Matthew. I'm not mad at you. You know that, right? I know I look frustrated, and I am. But not with you. I want you to know that. Okay? Okay."

I was confused but I chalked it up to my failure to understand what it was like to be an unmarried, middle-aged Baptist woman.

When Ms. Lansing opened her eyes, she snatched her purse off the floor, which made me nervous and excited at the same time. Was she going for her razor blades? Though I didn't want her to hurt herself, or anybody for that matter, I'd be lying if I didn't say I was a little disappointed when she pulled out a pen and a tablet of paper. It killed the mood in the room.

"What are you going to do?" I asked.

"I'm writing down what you said."

"Which part of what I said?"

"The stuff about Enya, New Age music, and pennywhistles."

"Why are you writing it down?"

"Because I'm going to have a little chat with Pastor Nolan, that's why." She put the pen behind her ear and moved back to her teacher's chair. "This is the third or fourth incident in the last two weeks. Somebody needs to fight for the creative people in this church."

"What are you fighting for?"

"For your imagination, Matthew. Without the imaginations of artists, the church will die or lose its ability to help people. I believe that."

I took my seat on the piano bench as Ms. Lansing grabbed the hymnal off the piano.

"Let's practice a different song. 'Work, for the Night Is Coming' makes me feel like I've been sentenced to hard labor in Siberia."

I smiled. That's when I tasted it for the first time: oatmeal with a hint of brown sugar.

For a lot of Christians, their imaginations are liabilities, like the five senses and genitals. Growing up in a church that bordered on being a religious regime often stole my chances to experience God as a mystery. Ms. Lansing told us that God made people creative so we could retell his story in new ways. She said it was a part of our calling. "You'll understand it in time," she said. "Trust me. God will make it clear when he needs your imagination."

A few months later, I received my first creative assignment from God while Mom and I were shopping at the Dover Mall. As she browsed through a rack of Looney Tunes T-shirts, I knelt beside a section of pink Tasmanian Devil tank tops, begging her to donate to the "Make Matthew Feel Good About Himself" fund. Against her better judgment, she handed me a twenty-dollar bill.

"You will not be sorry," I said, standing up and rubbing my knees free of the pain of spending fifteen minutes prayerfully following my mom around Strawbridge's. Mom's charitable donation was going to a worthy cause, though. I was convinced wearing the words *Coca-Cola* across my chest would make me very happy.

Mom continued shopping as I went and found a checkout counter. As I waited my turn, a song began playing over the store's sound system in which a male voice sang the word *faith* three times, really fast.

My interest piqued, I listened and waited for the chorus to come around again to make sure I had heard the singer correctly. I had. The man was definitely singing about faith, but I didn't know which faith he was singing about. It was the late eighties, which meant he could have been singing about Catholicism, Buddhism, or relativism. Even so, it was worth researching, just in case the song related the thrills of being born-again Baptist.

All I remembered was a small part of the chorus. When around somebody I thought was knowledgeable about or had contact with the secular world, I sang what I remembered, but learning who performed the song wasn't easy when the only people you knew were other Baptists.

Then my father introduced me to Sam, a thirty-something single man who had recently converted from being Episcopalian to Christianity. Since Sam wore black leather and drove a motorcycle to church, I figured I had a decent chance he might have heard the song prior to becoming one of God's children. One Sunday morning between Sunday school and church, I mustered up the courage to sing him the part of the chorus that I knew.

"Yeah, I know that song," he said.

"*Really?* That's awesome. Do you know who sings it?"

"Uh, George Michael. Why?"

"Well," I said, writing "George Michael" on my Sunday bulletin, "I've been curious to find out if the singer is a Christian. You know, because the song is about faith and all and…"

Sam rolled his eyes. "George Michael isn't a Christian."

"He isn't? I was afraid of that. He's a Jehovah's Witness, isn't he?"

"No."

"Hmm. Is he Buddhist?"

He shook his head.

"Is he Russian Orthodox?"

"No, man, he's bisexual."

"*Bisexual?* Is that an Eastern religion?"

Sam shrugged. "I don't know. It may be for some."

I didn't know the meaning of "bisexual." I didn't know if it was a religion or a disease or if it was similar to being ambidextrous. I thought people who could write with both their right and left hands were cool. They were always the biggest braggers in church, but they were easy to sit next to in the cafeteria.

"It means he's a…" Sam leaned in close so he could whisper, "a pervert. He likes women *and* men. Really *likes* them. You catchin' my drift?"

"Oh," I said, still unsure what he was getting at. "But is the song about his faith?"

"Maybe faith in his lover's body."

I felt embarrassed that I asked Sam about the song, but on the way home from church, God plopped an idea inside my head.

"MATTHEW!" said God, "I WANT YOU TO REWRITE THE LYRICS TO 'FAITH' TO MAKE THEM HOLY!"

"You want me to make them Baptist?" I asked.

"WELL," said God, "I WANT YOU TO MAKE THEM ABOUT ME."

So that's what I did; I rewrote the lyrics to "Faith" to make them about God. The chorus to my version went like this: *Gotta have faith in my Jesus, gotta have faith in my Lord. Gotta have faith, faith, faith.*

When I finished writing the new "born again" lyrics, I performed the song for my mother in our living room. She gushed, partly because she didn't know George Michael, but also because she liked my rhyming the words *God* and *sod.*

After hearing the new version, Mom suggested I sing it for my youth pastor, Mr. Billings, in the hope that he might use it in youth group. He liked my version of the song better than the original, but unfortunately he said he couldn't use it in youth group.

Apparently, though "Faith" no longer talked about a vile, sex-ridden faith and instead promoted a Jesus-filled faith, Mr. Billings feared a first-time visitor might hear us singing the familiar tune and think our church supported George Michael's promiscuous ways—both of them.

I didn't like Mr. Billings's decision, but it was consistent with my church's unadvertised slogan: "God may forget the sins of your past, but we never will!" George Michael could have become a Baptist missionary who fed starving babies in the Congo, but we would have always thought of him as one of those equal-opportunity guys looking for a little "wham."

In hindsight, I'm not sure God wanted me to rewrite the lyrics to "Faith." Perhaps I heard him wrong. Or maybe Ms. Lansing's passion got me so caught up in the excitement of receiving a "creative God assignment" that my imagination played the role of God's voice in my head. Or maybe I was bipolar before it became popular.

Fortunately, "Faith" was the only pop song I ever converted to Baptist. I think it was God's grace that my "Faith" didn't score the exposure I hoped it would, but the experience did spark my interest in songwriting.

I started carrying around a special notebook, and whenever I felt inspired to share my life in rhyme, I'd write. Most of what I wrote made stealing George Michael's song idea seem rather genius. Perhaps the most memorable lyric I wrote was about God receiving praise from cheetahs. In high school I had an odd fascination for large wild cats, but especially the cheetah. Other than my use of the word *pita* to rhyme with cheetah, the best part of the song happened in the chorus, which included the "word" *grrr*. In my mind, it just made sense that cheetahs would growl unto God once in a while.

My songs weren't works of art, but they were my works. I wrote about good things, bad things, and sometimes things I didn't know anything about. Whatever my imagination dreamed up, I wrote it down.

And it always rhymed.

On a day when I felt brave and more talkative than usual, I told Ms. Lansing about my new hobby of writing songs. Covering her mouth with her hand, she became so excited that tears started bubbling out of her eyes.

"That makes me so happy, Matthew. We need dreamers who use their imaginations. People like that keep Jesus alive." A coy grin cracked across her pale face. "Figuratively speaking, of course."

I sat down on the piano bench and flipped through the hymnal, looking for "O for a Thousand Tongues to Sing."

"But, Ms. Lansing," I said, "I can understand why some people don't use their imaginations."

"Why is that?"

"Because it gets you in trouble sometimes." I told her about rewriting the George Michael song.

At first she laughed. Then she lectured me about not using other people's creative work unless I was doing a parody. She added, "And don't do it unless it's really funny." But then, patting me on the back, she said, "But you're right; my imagination has gotten me into trouble on a number of occasions."

I placed the hymnal on the piano and looked at Ms. Lansing.

"People who play it safe rarely accomplish much," she said. "I doubt we would be sitting here talking about George Michael if he had played it safe."

"That makes sense," I said, putting my fingers on the first notes of "O for a Thousand Tongues to Sing." I banged through the first six chords and then stopped. I stopped and started three more times. Then I looked at Ms. Lansing, wondering why she hadn't yelled "Choppy!" and pushed me off the piano bench.

She didn't say anything. She just smiled faintly and nodded her head, a signal to keep trying.

I turned back to the piano, hit another bad chord, and sighed.

"Do you think I'd be any better at the pennywhistle?"

Bad for God

I've been told all my life that God's timing is perfect. And I believe that, for the most part. But on the afternoon he called me to become the Michael Jackson of Christian music, his "perfect timing" was tolerable at best.

My family and I were at Sea World in Orlando, watching trained sea lions play volleyball. I was sixteen, and before then, I'd never witnessed aquatic mammals bump, set, and spike. When one team of sea lions was finally deemed the winners, their trainer held up a bucket of fish and tossed minnows in both the winners' and losers' mouths.

"Okay, Sea World guests, we have a very special treat for you this afternoon!" A man wearing khaki shorts and a blue Sea World polo shirt looked back at one of his fellow trainers, and she gave him a nod. "Without further ado, please give a loud Sea World welcome to our newest little friend here at Sea World Orlando—Ollie!"

As soon as he said "Ollie," a loud beat that sounded like popcorn popping in rhythm started thumping out of the loudspeakers. Immediately, my sister's face turned ghostly white, which meant God was telling her something. Covering her ears with her hands, Elisabeth nudged me with her elbow.

"Cover your ears," she said in her demanding Christlike tone. "That is a syncopated beat if I ever heard one."

Elisabeth was right. The beat was syncopated, and for a young Independent Fundamental Baptist, few things existed that were more frightful than a syncopated beat. For good reason too.

Whenever my church deemed a beat "syncopated," it meant it was the kind of beat to which Baptist missionaries had witnessed evil spirits conjured among naked African tribes. That was why we covered our ears—just in case some of them tried to shimmy their way inside our heads. Demons were scary enough, but nude demons gyrating their hips inside our brains—that would require a prescription. And Baptists who required antidepressants often turned into atheists or, sometimes, Methodists.

I didn't want to be either, but the thought of standing among a bunch of strangers with my ears covered sounded immature. My sister was thirteen and on fire for Jesus, which made her incapable of stomaching guilt of any kind. I didn't like guilt either, but by the time I was in the eleventh grade, I believed I had mastered it to some degree. Not only could I hold my girlfriend's hand without confessing my sin to Youth Pastor Billings, I could tell my mother a white lie once in a while without getting diarrhea. That was as *free-in-Christ* as it got.

The music became louder, the rhythm heavier. All of us watched the stage with weighted anticipation for Ollie to appear. Then a voice that sounded familiar began singing over the beat. I knew the voice, but I couldn't place it.

Elisabeth elbowed me again. "Cover. Your. *Ears.*"

I glared at her but clapped my hands over my ears.

I looked around the crowded bleachers to see if anybody else was covering their ears. Sticking out like a sore thumb had one advantage—often it gave us the opportunity to meet other Independent Fundamental Baptists. It was encouraging to meet strangers, knowing that one day, we'd spend eternity together and they might end up owning the mansion next to ours in heaven. Those impromptu encounters with fellow "fundies" usually concluded with somebody saying, "It's so nice meeting you. If we don't meet again here on earth, we'll see you in heaven." And we replied, "Yes, and what a day of rejoicing that will be."

Scanning the bleachers, the only person I saw covering his ears was a man in the wheelchair section. But he was old and wearing a tank top, so I assumed he wasn't doing it because he was Baptist.

The first time I remember my mother making my sister and me "put our ear muffs on" happened during a trip to Drug Fair when the three of us heard Madonna for the first time. I was ten and didn't know what a virgin was, and by the look of repugnance on my mother's face, I was pretty sure I never wanted to find out. *It must be like the mumps or impetigo,* I thought.

As I stood in the bleachers, a small door on the left side of the stage opened, and the cutest furry animal I had ever seen appeared. Ollie was an otter. A *real* otter. The little guy pranced out to the beat of the music like he'd practiced his routine a thousand times. I had no idea that otters, like chimps, seals, and toddlers, could be trained to entertain humans. I wanted to applaud for Ollie, but I couldn't—not without unmuffling my ears. I considered asking the lady next to me if she minded putting her hands over my ears so I could clap, but she avoided eye contact.

Ollie scurried toward his trainer on his hind legs. In his little hands, he carried a Pepsi can, and it dawned on me how I knew the song: it was "Bad" from Michael Jackson's Pepsi commercial.

I'd only seen the ad a couple of times, but I loved it. The tune was so catchy; I couldn't deny its power over me. Its sound was so distinct. Even at muffled volume, the pop percussion and sensuous bass line took control of my head and made it bounce like a souped-up lowrider with hydraulics.

While the song played, Ollie did several tricks. He caught a ball. Waved at us in the bleachers. He even moonwalked. Three minutes into Ollie's act, I started wishing I were a small aquatic mammal that entertained strangers with waving or moonwalking or perhaps…

And that's when God spoke. Not audibly. Not with flaming clouds or burning shrubbery. Just in my head.

What if I become God's Michael Jackson? I thought. *That's just brilliant.*

I imagined God's Michael Jackson being exactly like the devil's Michael Jackson, except without catchy drumbeats, sexual dancing, and changing skin color. God told me that Baptists needed somebody to look up to, somebody talented who didn't wear a three-piece suit. Somebody they could listen to without guilt and still feel cool. God needed me.

As I thought about my idea, a peaceful satisfaction settled in my soul. I looked up into the sky and whispered, "Thank you, God. You never cease to amaze me."

I knew that seeing Ollie's dance performance wasn't by accident. God wanted me to see him shake his little abdomen. I knew because I didn't feel guilty for enjoying it.

When the show was over, as my family and I exited the amphitheater, I started singing "Bad" to myself. I had no idea what Michael

Jackson was saying in certain places, but I was pretty sure I knew the chorus:

You know I'm bad, I'm bad. She mall. You know I'm bad, I'm bad. She bald… And the whole world has to watermelon watermelon watermelon…
Who's bad?

When I got to the end of the chorus, I shot both of my arms up in the air. It just seemed like the thing to do.

"You wanna know who I think is bad?" said my friend Willie. "*Michael Jackson,* that's who." Willie rolled his eyes and shook his head at me.

Willie and I were the only two people in our homeroom class-room after school. He was there serving detention. One of the teachers heard him utter the word *golly* with the same inflection that sinners said the word *God.* I was making up an exam I had missed while on vacation. When I finished the test, I told Willie about what happened at Sea World and how it caused me to ponder if Baptists needed a Michael Jackson.

He thought the idea was ludicrous. "Why would Baptists need their own Michael Jackson, Matthew?"

"Why not?" I replied.

"You know what the Bible says as well as I do: whatsoever things are of *good report.* We're supposed to think on *those* things." He tapped his pointer finger against the table. "Michael Jackson is not of good report, Matthew."

"It's not like I would do the bad stuff that Michael Jackson does. You have to admit, there's something a little cool about him."

Willie's eyes grew to the size of Egg McMuffins.

"Do you hear yourself? There is nothing holy, upright, *or* cool about Michael Jackson. Nothing. He's a sinner." Willie quieted his voice to a whisper. "He grabs his private area when he sings. I suppose you think that's what God has called you to do?"

He was joking, but both of us immediately thought of our Algebra II instructor, Mr. Nelg. In addition to teaching us about polynomials and factoring, Mr. Nelg also taught the high school boys' Sunday school class. The year before, he'd spent forty-five minutes talking to us about how disgusted he was that Michael Jackson grabbed his crotch in front of teenagers.

"Can you imagine?" he said. "If I ever caught one of you young men grabbing *down there* in public"—he lowered his eyes for emphasis—"I would come up behind you and kick you in the backside."

Normally, when Mr. Nelg wandered onto one of his off-topic discussions, it was sort of interesting. At least more interesting than the Bible story he was supposed to be teaching us. But having to sit and listen straight-faced to his tirade about Michael Jackson's lack of good tact bordered on unmerciful. His point was valid, but it seemed a bit hypocritical, considering Mr. Nelg picked and pulled at his *down there* all the time. We told ourselves his habit was different than Michael Jackson's, because for him, it was something he did when he was nervous or uncomfortable; Michael Jackson did it on stage in front of thousands of people.

I quickly realized that debating the validity of what God had told me with Willie was pointless, so I asked, "Willie, do you ever hear God?"

Willie rolled his eyes, and I knew why. As much as my friends and I talked about God, the Bible, and all the various things that God mentioned he hated in the Bible, we rarely spoke aloud about how

God interacted with us personally. It just wasn't a topic that got brought up.

Which meant that when it did get brought up, we didn't know how to respond honestly. We talked all the time about how God was close to us. We even knew the proper way in which to explain it. Our bodies are the temples of God, we told non-Baptists. As one of God's temples, we were like walking church sanctuaries that he lived inside. But none of us seemed *close* to God. We just told people we were.

"Sometimes I think he says things to me," Willie said. "But to be honest, I don't really know what his voice sounds like. Most of the time it seems there are a whole bunch of voices sounding off in my head. Do you know what he sounds like?"

I shrugged my shoulders. "I don't know for sure. The voice I hear sounds British."

Willie crinkled his face up into a scowl. "British? That's definitely not the voice I hear. Why would God have a British accent? I could see a Jewish accent, but not British."

I'm not sure why, but in my mind God usually spoke like a proper Englishman. Perhaps it was because I thought British people sounded more intelligent than Americans. Or maybe it was because the actors in most movies loosely based on the Bible always sounded odd and stuffy, like they held teacups with their pinkies out.

"Well," I said, "does the voice that you think is God's ever tell you what you should do when you grow up?"

"Yep. I'm either going to be a fireman or an emergency medical technician. It's like God can't make up his mind, so I keep going back and forth between the two."

Willie was right. God sometimes seemed a bit schizophrenic when it came to helping people make decisions regarding careers. In my short life, he'd told me to be a veterinarian, a pharmacist, Jerry Falwell's choir director, a psychiatrist, and a preacher willing to move to Sweden. Now he was telling me to be Michael Jackson so Christians would have somebody to idolize.

"You've wanted to work in rescue since you were a kid, huh?"

"Pretty much. That, and hunt. I did go through a preacher phase when I was ten, but it passed."

"I've always enjoyed music, so maybe that's what I'm supposed to do."

"But don't you think there's a big difference between singing solos in church and being like Michael Jackson?"

Willie didn't seem to understand what I was trying to say, and I wasn't very good at explaining it. Two years went by before I mentioned it again, but I never stopped thinking about it. I kept hearing God say it over and over in my head.

"Ye kno wut yur supoozed t' do, Matthew. Kreesjun mewssic needs a Meekle Jooksin."

Sometimes God sounded like he was from Russia. Or Boston. Either way, he was hard to understand sometimes.

When I was a senior in high school, the first question most people asked when the topic of college came up was something like, "So, Matthew, what do you want to do with the rest of your life?"

An odd sensation came over my body whenever I was asked that. The hairs all over my body stood at attention and shook fearfully, while my neck tightened with anxiety.

"Uh, well," I said, "it's sort of complicated."

Complicated was a good word to use in that situation, because most people responded by nodding and saying something along the lines of, "You don't have to say another word, Matthew. I understand. It is complicated. Figuring out what you want to do with your life can be stressful. It was for me. But you'll figure it out. God will show you what you should do. You'll see."

But the people who asked me that question had no clue about my dilemma. They didn't understand what made my situation complicated. My problem had nothing to do with not knowing what I was going to do with the rest of my life. My problem was that I thought God had revealed exactly what I was supposed to do, and I didn't want to tell anybody about it.

I wasn't ashamed of my spiritual calling, but admitting I planned to move to Nashville because God had called me to be the Michael Jackson of Christian music wasn't easy. People looked at me exactly how one might expect them to look at somebody who said out loud that he wanted to be the Michael Jackson of Christian music. I imagined I would have gotten the same reaction if I'd been standing in front of them wearing a pink tutu and singing "*She's* Got the Whole World in Her Hands."

Some people became defensive. Some quoted Scripture. Others laughed. Some changed the subject. Once in a while they asked questions:

Does Christian music need a Michael Jackson?

Can you moonwalk?

Will you wear a glove on one hand? Which one?

Does Nashville know you're coming?

The negativity and sarcasm overwhelmed me at times, but I wasn't surprised by it.

Any time God was involved in somebody's circumstances, Baptists expected a fair amount of teasing and mocking. That was especially true when God's involvement regarded one's calling. It was practically a given. Whenever God chose somebody to do something miraculous or special or asinine, Pastor Nolan told us to anticipate scoffers. He said scoffers could come from anywhere—work, home, even church.

I pictured scoffers coming at me like the Philistines came at the Israelites in the Bible. They didn't carry spears and swords like the Philistines. They usually came carrying Bibles under their arms or stories of fear on their tongues.

But there was a bright side to being scoffed at; it sometimes meant Satan didn't like you or your plan.

"Satan doesn't waste his time on anything that God isn't behind," Pastor Nolan said. "So facing the scorn of others is like God stamping his approval on your idea."

Since almost everybody I told mocked my calling, I figured God must have really wanted me to be the Michael Jackson of Christian music.

Pastor Nolan did try to encourage us with pep talks once in a while. He told us that whenever people criticized or stood in the way of our callings, we should keep our eyes on the mission God set before us and run over the cynics and pessimists as if they were merely speed bumps.

"When God calls you to do something," he preached on several occasions, "you don't stop when people mock you or say mean things about you. You don't stop doing God's work for nobody! You keep going."

Sometimes Pastor Nolan offered us examples of people in the Bible who didn't stop. "Moses didn't stop when the children of Israel complained! Joshua didn't stop when the Israelites whined about walking around the city of Jericho! Noah didn't stop when people teased him about building the ark!"

Out of Pastor Nolan's three examples, I identified a lot with Noah. His story seemed to be the most outrageous to me. Back then I had a great appreciation for the biblically outrageous. The crazier a Bible story seemed, the more hope I found in God's ability to do something big and crazy in my life.

Noah's circumstances and mine were quite different, though. God hadn't called him to become a Baptist-based King of Popular Christian Music, and I had no intention of waiting 120 years for God to fulfill that destiny. My father told me that if something didn't happen by the time I finished my degree, he would find me a job at Maryland's Department of Agriculture. Dad said four years was plenty of time for God to recognize whether or not a man's faith was up to par, and after that it was time to settle down and get a real job.

Another difference was that, unlike Noah's, my calling didn't come with an apocalypse attached. One friend disagreed. He told me that my becoming a combo of Michael Jackson and Jesus was definitely a sign of The End.

I understood what it felt like to be mocked simply because I was following God's call on my life.

My favorite part of Pastor Nolan's encouragement was the conclusion. He'd stop screaming, look around the auditorium, wipe beads of sweat off his forehead, and then whisper, "But the naysayers who mocked Moses, Joshua, and Noah didn't get the last laugh. No, they didn't. Does anybody know who did? Church, are you listening to me this morning? Who got the last laugh?"

People in the auditorium usually got excited during this part. Some would holler, "Amen" or "Preach it" or "I know who laughed, Pastor." Others nodded their heads and fanned their faces with church bulletins. And then Pastor Nolan delivered his grand finale.

"You wanna know who got the last laugh, Church?" he said, his voice becoming louder with each word. "Moses got the last laugh. Joshua got the last laugh! NOAH got the last laugh! And ultimately, GOD GOT THE LAST LAUGH!"

Whenever Pastor Nolan preached that sermon, I always left church wanting to laugh—just like Moses, Joshua, Noah, and God laughed. So far everybody else was laughing, but I was confident I would get my chance: in God's perfect time.

Different Places, Same World

If you don't stop singing, Matthew, I swear I'm going to…" My pseudo-friend Roberta grimaced, not because she minded my singing voice, but because she loathed the song.

She was a strange fundamentalist in a lot of ways, at least, compared to the ones I knew. Unlike most of the people at my church, Roberta didn't have the personality or patience for emotional thrills. She didn't like puppy posters with Scripture verses on them or Precious Moments statues or reruns of *Highway to Heaven*. Even though we had gone to school together for six years and graduated in the same class, I still wondered if I actually knew her. At times the walls Roberta put up between her and the rest of the world were so thick, so unnatural, that I got the impression her emotions might have been missing a part or two. I got a similar feeling whenever I saw Liza Minnelli's eyes. Whenever I saw Liza on television, her eyes always seemed like they worked too hard to appear normal. Thankfully, like Liza's eyes, the only time I noticed something strange about Roberta's emotions happened when I got too close.

"If I continue singing, Roberta, what are you going to do?" I raised my eyebrows and tried hard to appear serious. "Hit me?"

"I might," she said, with a devilish grin. "So don't mess with me. You know I hate sappy God songs, especially ones that sound like love songs."

"It is a love song, Roberta." I smiled, thinking about the numerous occasions I tortured her in high school by sitting behind her in various classes and whispering in her ear the lyrics to songs that weren't hymns. "But it's meant to be a love song to God. Or at least about God."

"Please. Spare me the explanation, Matthew." Roberta's brown eyes fixed on me through the plastic-framed glasses that kept sliding down her oily nose. Each time, Roberta pushed them back up with her middle finger, perhaps her subconscious offering me a message of its own. "Why anybody would want to sing a love song to God, I'll never know."

The song that Roberta hated was "Place in This World." Among Christians who weren't Independent Fundamental Baptists, the song was quite popular. Written and performed by Michael W. Smith, a Christian pop star famous for piano-driven torch songs to Jesus, "Place in This World" showcased Michael telling somebody—I assumed God—that he needed them to help him find his purpose in life or "place in this world." The song's lyrics never referred to God or Jesus directly, but all the pronouns pointed to God.

I was a huge fan of Smitty. "Smitty" was the name all his famous friends called him—people like Amy Grant, Gary Chapman, Wayne Kirkpatrick, and others. Maybe his mother. Members of his fan club called him that too. Once I became his fan, I wanted to be able to refer to Michael as Smitty too. As soon as I turned eighteen, old enough to join the Michael W. Smith Fan Club without my mother's permission, I sent my registration card and twenty-five dollars to a PO box in Nashville. Six to eight weeks later, I received a letter in the mail informing me that I was an official fan. Immediately, I wrote him a fan letter:

> Dear Smitty,
>   I am one of your biggest fans. That's not easy at my church. Some people think that listening to your music will send me to hell. But I think they're just jealous because you're popular and they're not. Anyway, I hope I get to meet you someday. That would be awesome!
>   Sincerely, in Christ,
>   Matthew Turner

Talking to Roberta, I was unwilling to let the topic die. I said, "Some people like being emotionally vulnerable with God. It makes them feel closer to him and their relationship more personal, more real."

Roberta didn't say anything. She rolled her eyes and tore the cellophane off a brand-new roll of masking tape with her teeth.

Home on summer break from the Florida prison she called a Christian Bible college, Roberta had called and asked if I would help decorate the church auditorium for the annual Fourth of July service. Why she thought to call me, I wasn't sure. The two of us weren't exactly adversaries in high school, but we weren't BFFs either. Usually I used the same avoidance tactics in my relationship with Roberta that most species applied to crocodiles or atheists.

Nevertheless, I found myself at church with Roberta, getting ready to hang red, white, and blue streamers on the church's altar. At IBBC only Easter trumped the Fourth of July in popularity, and it was our responsibility to make the church auditorium look as gaudy as a parade float.

"Vulnerable schmulnerable." Roberta pulled her straw-colored hair back, held it like a ponytail for a few seconds, and then let it go. "As far as I'm concerned, it's just childish spirituality—watered-down Christianity!"

I don't know why I felt the need to argue with Roberta, but I did. I wasn't very good at it. I was much more equipped to argue her side than mine. I'd argued her side for as long as I could remember.

But over the previous year, since graduating from high school, I'd started discovering a little grace in my Christianity. Not pure grace, but for me it felt like a spiritual revolution. My grace—little more than the freedom to listen to electric guitar solos and read books by C. S. Lewis—was a new and scary experience. A person's first steps into grace are usually unsettling, more like walking into a minefield than a meadow. Still, whenever I was around die-hard fundamentalists like Roberta, knowing grace made me feel like I had secret powers. So I argued a lot. It was my way of practicing how to properly use my powers. I did sometimes feel sorry for my opponent—not because I was educated on the topic, but because I was not. It could be hard to argue with someone who didn't actually know what he was talking about.

"Roberta, getting emotional with God is not watered-down Christianity."

"I'll put it this way, Matthew. I don't need to sing a worldly love song to make God aware of my love or need for him." Roberta tore open the bag of streamers and handed me the loose end of a red roll.

Holding it between my fingers, I grabbed the roll of tape and began tearing off small pieces and sticking them all over my pant leg.

"What makes it worldly, Roberta?"

Roberta gripped her hair again.

"I really don't want to talk about this anymore, Matthew. It's just making me angry. You keep your pop songs to yourself, and I'll stick to hymns, thank you very much. Now, let's hang these streamers."

College hadn't changed Roberta one bit. Which made sense because nobody expected it to change her. Not at the institution she went to. The college she attended might boast palm trees and sunshine most of the year, but beyond the marketing brochure, it was far better known for being a boarding school for aspiring zealots—and Roberta was the ideal candidate.

During our senior year, she and I, along with two other classmates, Willie and Mason, attended a college weekend at her school. The admissions office paid for our visit, and Willie, Mason, and I only went because it was free trip to Florida. But it was nice to discover that all the rumors we had heard were true.

The school did have *his*-and-*her* sidewalks. Students weren't allowed off campus with any member of the opposite sex without a chaperone. And the school's elevators were gender specific too—just in case a dating couple got the wise idea to push the emergency-stop button between floors and touch hands.

Roberta and I finished hanging the decorations. Standing in the back of the auditorium, we inspected our work. In my opinion the church altars looked perfectly patriotic, like red, white, and blue sacrifices unto God, worthy of a presidential inauguration. We'd created the perfect backdrop for Sunday's Declaration of Independence Service.

When Roberta deemed our decorating complete, we decided to walk across the street to our town's strip mall for lunch.

As we walked, I continued to beat the dead horse by once again mumble-singing "Place in This World."

"You're singing again, Matthew." Roberta spoke in a tone that communicated far more than her words did.

"How can you not like this song?" I looked at her like she belonged in a straitjacket. "It's a song to Jesus, Roberta. You *love* Jesus."

"How do you know it's about Jesus? I haven't heard you sing the name of God or Jesus."

"It's implied."

"Whatever, Matthew; that song could be talking about anybody." Roberta pointed at me. "And you know it."

Fundamentalists didn't like using pronouns in reference to God unless one of God's many names was used in the same sentence. Some thought God pronouns left too much to chance, while others believed that using "he" or "him" meant you were ashamed of the "he" or "him" you were referring to.

Roberta and I decided to eat at Chestertown's version of a New York–style pizza joint called Procolino's. It's the kind of restaurant you don't mind walking into even though you'll walk out smelling like body odor. Whatever they put on their pizzas and in their calzones, after a trip to Procolino's, I always smelled like a seventh grader who hadn't started using deodorant. But the pizza was great.

Sitting down at the table and looking over the menu, I said, "Roberta, don't you think the Holy Spirit can tell the difference between a song that's being sung to God and one that's not?"

"It doesn't matter whether the Holy Spirit *can* do that or not; I don't believe he should have to do that, Matthew. It's silly."

Roberta was the kind of Independent Fundamental Baptist who believed in the existence of the Holy Spirit, but she was under the assumption that he/she/it had retired at some point toward the end of the first century. After that, God didn't need the Holy Spirit.

A lot of people believed that at my church.

A few of those people believed that God contracted his spirit to be his eyes and ears in 1611 when King James commissioned translating the Bible from Hebrew and Greek to English. But those same people also believed that, in the places where the King James Version of the Bible differed from the original text, the original text was wrong, not the English version that God had reauthorized. They simply believed that the Holy Spirit came to the people of the seventeenth century and reinterpreted it in English, with 100 percent accuracy this time.

And then the Holy Spirit retired again.

"Let me ask you something, Matthew." Roberta glanced over her menu. "Why do we need God to communicate to us in the present when he gave us everything we needed to know in the past? You know, right here in his Word."

Roberta patted her Bible like it was a Chihuahua sleeping next to her place mat.

I can't remember Roberta ever walking out of her house without bringing along what she called "the only instruction manual I'll ever need." She believed the Bible had an answer for everything.

"I bring it along just in case," she'd say. "I never know when I'll need a quick fix of God's inspired words. You know what I mean? As far as I'm concerned, I carry the Holy Spirit with me. In my purse."

Our pizza arrived, and both of us grabbed a slice.

"Wait a minute. Don't you think there's a chance that God might speak to us now?" I pulled a napkin from the dispenser on the table and patted off all the visible grease from my pizza. "It makes no sense that God would be so vocal for thousands of years and then just stop talking."

"Of course he speaks to us, Matthew," she said. "But only through this book." She massaged the back of her Bible again. "That's all he'll ever say to us until we hear the trumpet sound and get called up into heaven."

Roberta talked about God like a scientist talked about gravity or Darwin, with no room for mystery or wonder.

The conversation lulled as we chewed our pizza. I thought about the last time Roberta and I saw each other.

For Halloween our church had converted an old, deserted farm-house into what the youth director, Pastor Eric, called God's Little House of Eternal Torment and Shame. He smiled as he described to parents a haunted house that he believed Jesus would design had he stuck around long enough to experience Halloween.

I laughed when he told me what he was calling it. I knew a few churches that could have gone by the same name.

To those who disagreed with him, Pastor Eric said, "Your kids are teenagers now! Singing 'Jesus Loves the Little Children' just doesn't cut it anymore."

Like everybody in my church, I was concerned for the souls of

Kent County's teenagers, but I thought Pastor Eric's idea was fear-filled, strange, and a little too much like a regular Sunday service. But I was also interested in seeing how Jesus would scare the living daylights out of twelve- to sixteen-year-old heathens. I told Pastor Eric that I would volunteer, and he asked me to be one of Jesus's demons. I jumped at the opportunity. Roberta flew home from college for the event. She and her father were in charge of their own room, the finale of Jesus's House of Terror.

For ninety minutes I floated around the house, wearing camouflage garb and white makeup on my face, jumping out at random people from behind corners, doing my best to scare people into becoming friends with Jesus.

Roberta spent the evening chained to a piece of plywood, playing the role of a Christian woman ensnared by Satan and now being tortured by him. Mr. Langly, Roberta's father, played Satan. His portrayal was better than I anticipated. He was shorter than I imagined Satan being, and more tan, but like Ozzy Osbourne, Mr. Langly was quite good at growling and gnashing his teeth.

During Roberta's fourth performance, I took a breather from being one of Pastor Eric's evil agents and decided to walk through God's Crazy House as though I were a lost soul looking for hope. During the twenty-minute walk-through, I witnessed the decapitation of an angel, a demon performing an abortion, and two rock'n'roll lovers dying of a drug overdose. Hope was frightening. Roberta's performance impressed me with her acting ability. Her portrayal of a tortured young saint of God was believable. Her body was covered with fake blood, and her ability to scream was Oscar-worthy.

But midway through, her performance took a strange turn. Rather than sticking with the bloody-murder screams of terror she was so good at, Roberta began yelling passages of Scripture at Satan.

"You don't have to live like this, Satan. 'Trust in the LORD with all of your heart; and lean not unto thine own understanding!'"

Roberta's muscles strained as she tried to loosen herself from Satan's chains. "You can be free. The Bible says so! Jesus says, 'For God so loved the world, that he gave his only begotten Son!'"

Oh my, I thought. Roberta was trying to get Satan to ask Jesus into his heart.

Satan got in her face. "Don't ever say that name around me! I hate the name of Jesus."

"But, Devil," Roberta yelled, *"PLEASE!* You could be free of this evil! The wages of sin is death, but the gift of God is eternal life! You could have eternal life. There's still time."

"I want nothing to do with your petty God, woman!" Satan punched Roberta in the face.

Or he pretended to. Roberta's performance was so convincing that I really believed Satan had just hit her.

"I am my own god!" Satan picked up his chain saw and, with one pull of the string, started it.

"Don't do this Satan! God loves you. Don't do this! You can save yourself from the eternal torment of sin! There's still time, Lucifer! There's still time!"

Satan swung the chain saw in front of her face. "I'm gonna cut you into a hundred pieces!"

As Roberta screamed and begged for her life to be spared, Satan thrust the chain saw into the plywood wall she was tied to. And that's when I noticed—*oh my gosh, Satan didn't take the chain off the chain saw*—and I gasped. But it was too late. Satan lost control of his weapon and the blade sawed across the lower part of Roberta's arm, creating a gash the size of a Band-Aid. Blood began pouring out of Roberta's arm. The audience around me, unaware of what just occurred, hooted and applauded.

Satan leaned over Roberta's face. The two whispered a few sentences to each other, and then Roberta nodded her head, telling Satan she wanted to continue her performance of the plan of salvation.

Roberta yelled some more sentences about how much Jesus loved Satan, and that he had died for his sins too. The act was a bit much, even for Baptists, but Roberta's stamina—mainly resisting fainting due to blood loss—was quite impressive. Of course, the scene offered about as much good theology as one of those cheerleading horror flicks, where a dippy blonde with big boobs and pompoms gets knocked off every seven minutes.

Eventually somebody called 911, an ambulance arrived, and Satan held Roberta's hand as the two rode to the hospital together.

Putting another slice of pizza on my plate, I asked, "How's your arm?"

"It's doing okay," Roberta said, looking down at the four-by-one-inch scar under her left elbow.

For some reason I didn't believe her. I could tell it was an uncomfortable subject for her to talk about.

"My fingers tingle sometimes, and it still hurts to touch. But the doctor believes the pain and the tingles will eventually disappear."

"Explain to me why you kept playing the role after your father gashed you with a chain saw."

"Something inside of me told me to keep going. I had to continue. And I'm glad I did." Roberta peeled a pepperoni off the top of her pizza and dropped it in her mouth. She grinned at me awkwardly. "It was worth it to me, because one person met Jesus from that performance. If I stopped in the middle of the scene, that might not have happened. It was just a little gash."

Just a little gash. I shook my head.

It dawned on me that I would never fully understand Roberta. I wanted to understand her, but only if she would understand me in return. At the time, that only seemed fair. But the chances of that happening were slim. Our brand of Baptist wasn't known for teaching mutual understanding. It was common for two or more Baptists to gather in circles to debate and argue until everybody agreed or they turned into enemies.

I didn't want to be Roberta's enemy. I didn't want to be her best friend either, but what was wrong with hoping for reciprocated respect?

I knew it wouldn't be an easy feat, mostly because I thought Roberta was nuts. She didn't like being emotional with God, and she was convinced that God's spirit was confined to the pages of the Bible she carried in her pocketbook. She continued to play the part of a tortured woman after "Satan" nearly cut off her arm with a chain saw.

And she hated Michael W. Smith without even giving his song a chance.

I was too tired to continue trying to convince her she was wrong and I was right. I didn't know which one of us was right. Perhaps the

Holy Spirit *was* resting in her purse next to a tube of lipstick. I didn't know.

I was learning that I didn't know a lot of things. And I think a part of faith is learning how to become okay with that.

Famous, Twice Removed

The moment I laid eyes on the long leather coats that brothers Jack and Jeff Gladstone wore over their collarless dress shirts and the thin gold sunglasses that framed their faces, I knew I wanted to be friends with them. The brothers dressed like Johnny Cash, which I assumed—along with most of the people at IBBC—meant they were famous.

I didn't have any famous friends, but I certainly dreamed about befriending people with notoriety. Like souvenirs, I wanted a collection of them. Becoming close acquaintances with people Jesus had deemed holy and talented enough to be his representation to ordinary, untalented pew dwellers seemed like a good way to get on Jesus's favorable side. Plus, I figured I could learn a thing or two about how to be a famous Christian.

Jack and Jeff's sister Jane was a member at IBBC, so the brothers felt comfortable with the congregation, and it didn't take long until they started talking about how it felt to be famous.

"It's amazing," said Jeff. A crowd of teenage girls in long skirts and white bobbysocks gathered around the younger of the two brothers like pigeons circling a half-eaten hot dog at an amusement park, clucking and cooing as he talked. "We just got off tour, so it's nice having a break and spending time with our sister."

Spread across the two or three pews in front of him, the flock of females seemed enamored with Jeff. They pecked at his every word. Was it his southern accent? His L.A. Looks–inspired mullet? His fame? The young pigeons didn't pay any attention to Jack, the older, taller, and bigger-boned brother. He had a different—more mature—group of fans.

"Yes ma'am, we're working on new music right now." Jack's ego puffed up as his chest puffed out, and the group of cougar-ish moms around him purred and growled.

The following Sunday, Pastor Nolan invited Jack, Jeff, and Jane to sing during the evening service. Jeff played guitar while his sister and brother belted out a couple of old southern gospel tunes—"Because He Lives" and "Glory to the Lamb." Before singing the second song, the brothers noted that it was nice to be reunited with Jane. The three of them had once traveled and sung together as the Poppa Gladstone Family Singers. Poppa Gladstone was their father, a traveling evangelist.

"We were sort of like the Jackson Five," Jane once told me, "except we sang southern gospel music."

What Jane didn't say was that nearly every musical act that sings southern gospel music is made up of family members who think of themselves as the Jackson Five, when in reality they were more like the Partridge Family—minus the tour bus, stage outfits, and weekly television show.

Since getting married, Jane had left the traveling life and started a family. She missed feeling famous. I could see the longing in her eyes when she sang solos or duets with her husband in church. Perfectly postured, with a microphone in her hand, Jane sang to us with a blank stare, as if imagining herself singing for thousands. Performing with Jack and Jeff again, Jane glowed with pride and self-worth, like she was making a comeback.

When my mother saw a similar gleam in my eye, she'd sit me down and talk to me about fame. "It's controlling," she said. "It gets into your system like a drug and it's hard not to want more—even when you didn't really have it in the first place."

I think Mom's warnings were as much for her as they were for me. Both of us were dreamers and quite enamored with our God-given abilities. We enjoyed sitting around and fantasizing about what we wanted to be when we grew up. Age and setting made my mother's dream of becoming a famous Bible teacher seem pointless to some people, but not to me.

"I could do that," she said whenever *The 700 Club* featured a woman talking eloquently about her God-experiences with co-host Sheila Walsh. "You know I could. I bet Sheila and I would be good friends. She seems like a person I could really like. All it would take is somebody giving me a chance, and I could be a fantastic Christian women's speaker and go on *The 700 Club*."

I never doubted that Mom could be famous for talking about God. She certainly talked about him enough. Mom was most expressive talking about him, and the tone she used when she spoke of spiritual things sounded exactly like the professionals—that unique ability to sound angelic, grounded, and condescending all at the same time.

"Do you understand what I'm talking about, Matthew? About the trouble with desiring popularity?" Mom asked at the end of those fame lectures.

I always nodded and told her I understood. But I also knew that I craved fame. I longed to be seen. Heard. Known. Loved.

When she finished talking, Mom would smile, hug my neck, and remind me again that she loved me. But sometimes I saw the worry in her eyes. Maybe that was because she knew fame had already gotten into my system. Or maybe she worried because she thought it could be hereditary.

It was difficult to not be impressed with Jack and Jeff. Their Holy Spirit–inspired charisma radiated off them like heat from a rash. Befriending them proved harder than I imagined, though. Not because I wasn't friendly toward them, but because there always seemed to be a feeding frenzy of pigeons and cougars surrounding them, hanging on every word, story, and exaggeration they dished out.

In the church parking lot one evening, I finally got the chance to talk to them.

"We're sort of in between careers," Jack told me when I asked what it was like being a famous Christian. "We used to be well known in southern gospel circles. Have you heard of the group Gold City Quartet?"

"You were in Gold City?"

"Oh, no. Not *in* Gold City, but we were almost as popular as they are. In certain states. We were called the Poppa Gladstone Family Singers," said Jeff.

"Yeah, I've heard your sister talk about the group. She says you're like the Jackson Five."

"Yeah?" Jack and Jeff said in unison, both grinning.

"Our father, Poppa Gladstone, is even more famous than we are," said Jack.

According to Jack and Jeff, Poppa Gladstone was all the rage in eastern Tennessee, southern Virginia, and Muncie, Indiana.

Later, when I told Dad the geographical locations of Jack and Jeff's fame, he laughed. "I could stand out in the middle of an empty field in my drawers and draw more people than those two and their daddy." Dad was the only member of our family unimpressed with the Gladstone family.

"Keep this between us," said Jeff, "but in most of West Virginia, Poppa's more popular than Billy Graham and Jerry Falwell."

"Wow, really?" I said. "Does your dad preach in football stadiums when he goes there?"

"Oh, no," Jeff said. "Poppa's too humble for any of that coliseum stuff. But he could, though. And we certainly wouldn't mind, that's for sure." Jeff nudged his brother in the side with his elbow. "Ain't that right?"

Jack looked like he was drooling, just thinking about it.

"But Poppa believes in preaching the gospel the old-fashioned way—tent revivals."

"*Tent revivals?*"

"Tent revivals."

The brothers decided to live in Kent County for a while, being between careers. Jeff wanted to finish his last year of high school at

IBBC's Christian school, and Jack enrolled at the community college I attended. It wasn't long before I started hanging out with Jack and Jeff outside of church. The brothers never came to my house. I always went to theirs and did whatever they already had planned. I went along with the arrangement because if I didn't, then we wouldn't hang out at all. I felt honored and privileged being one of the few people chosen to be in their circle of friends.

Going to college with Jack on Tuesdays and Thursdays made us closer. For some reason I felt like I needed his friendship. Living vicariously through his fame, I started feeling famous too.

"Matthew, we need to talk." My friend Kathy sounded alarmed. That worried me, because she was smarter than me, and I respected her emotional responses to most situations. She and I had met two summers before, when we worked at Masten Home Center. We only saw each other when she came home from college, and that summer we worked together at a lumberyard.

Kathy's goal was to get her PhD in Christian psychiatry and then move to a city with a large population of pastors who needed therapy and medication. Dallas or Houston, she thought. I was excited for her. Because of her degree, Kathy seemed to understand people, especially Christian people.

That first summer at the lumberyard, when I verbally judged another employee after he blurted out that he and his girlfriend had a party in their bedroom the night before, Kathy took me aside. After a good chiding, which included quoting Jesus, Mother Teresa, and Mr. Rogers, she eventually diagnosed me with faith-based narcissism.

"Wow, really?" I loved when Kathy used big words to describe my conditions. She seemed to think I had quite a few serious issues. I didn't understand half the words she used, but I enjoyed hearing her talk about me. "That sounds interesting. What is it?"

Kathy sighed loudly. "It *means* the relationship you have with your faith causes you to be rigid and functionally impaired, even maladaptive in some instances. The manner in which you integrate your model of Christianity into conversations and other people's realities reveals an unhealthy necessity for dominance and self-gratification. You become eccentric and often passively aggressive. I think Sigmund Freud would classify you as dysfunctional and socially malignant."

I looked at her across the pile of two-by-fours we were counting for inventory. "I'm like cancer?"

"Sort of. A treatable kind."

Anger began brewing in my brain. It was a biblical kind of anger, the kind where tablets made of stone got thrown off mountaintops and tables inside temples got turned over.

"Well, I don't know who this Freud person is," I said, "and frankly I don't care. He sounds like the type of person God might turn into a pillar of salt or slaughter and then have a pack of dogs eat his bones. I don't care what he thinks about me!"

"Never mind, Matthew."

The following year Kathy told me she saw significant improvement in the way I displayed my faith in public. When I told her that I sat between an atheist and a Roman Catholic in my statistics class, she seemed quite impressed.

When she called me this time, Kathy wanted to talk about my friendship with Jack and Jeff. She knew Jack and Jeff far better than I did because she'd been in love with Jack for three days. He'd loved her back for two of those days. The aftermath, which included phone calls, tears, weekend silent treatments, and five or six random make-out sessions, stretched over four months. But she swore the relationship was over now.

"You'd better be careful, Matthew." Kathy raked her plain brown hair with her fingers. "Jack and Jeff are blow-hards! Seriously, they practice being humble in the mirror. Their family will suck you in, and before you know it, you'll be eating out of their hands."

"Kathy," I said, "is this your broken heart talking?"

"My heart isn't broken, Matthew! You won't say that when the Gladstones find new people to extend their hands to."

I felt faint just thinking about the possibility. "Why would they do that? I'm not going anywhere."

"Because that's what they do. They act like they love you right up until you need them to love you. And then they leave. That's what they do. They feed off other people's attention. Like television evangelists."

I felt nauseated.

Two days after Kathy and I talked, I met Jack and Jeff for lunch. As I bit into a crispy chicken sandwich, Jack said, "We have some exciting news to tell you."

"What news?"

Jack turned his head toward Jeff. "You tell him."

"Well, Matthew," said Jeff enthusiastically, "Jack and I decided last night that God is calling us to become the next big Christian rock duo."

I'm sure the brothers could read the emotional slide show that flashed across my face. Shock. Curiosity. Thrill. My mind worked through a lengthy list of questions: *The two of you* decided *that God was calling you? Who's the current big Christian rock duo you'll be following? Can duos even rock? Would you consider making it a trio? Trios might rock.*

"*Sooooo,*" I said, "what kind of rock music are you guys planning to make?" I looked at Jeff, then Jack.

Jeff spoke up. "We've been thinking about it a lot, and our sound is gonna be sweet, man. Like Guns N' Roses meets Extreme. But acoustic."

I nodded like I knew what he was talking about. I didn't listen to Guns N' Roses because I wasn't allowed, and truthfully, it was never much of a temptation. The only Extreme song I knew was a single that got played over and over again on Baltimore's Mix 106.5. But the word *acoustic* I understood; it was Christian for "boring."

"The music will *rock*"—Jack raised his hand to offer me a high-five—"but all the lyrics will be about Jesus. I think we have a real chance to use this music to make a difference."

"We definitely have a chance of making it," said Jeff. "Our music is going to be stinkin' sweet! You'll get to hear some of it, eventually."

"Hey, why don't we give Matthew a taste of what we can do right now?" Jack looked at Jeff and grinned. Jeff nodded. I felt like I was costarring in an episode of *Saved by the Bell,* listening to Zack and Slater talk about their plans to get girls to go to Make-Out Point with them.

"Sounds good to me, my brother," said Jeff.

"Are you thinking what I'm thinking?"

Nodding, Jeff tapped three times on the table in front of him.

Then the two of them closed their eyes, and with their heads bobbing to the beat of the music in their heads, started singing: *"More than words…is all you have to do to make it real…then you wouldn't have to say…cause I'd already know…"*

For two and a half minutes, Jeff sang lead while Jack sang harmony. Jeff's tapping kept them in time, and Jack's right hand moved up and down with the melody. They were pretty good, especially when they harmonized their voices, but I would have liked them a lot better if we hadn't been sitting at Burger King.

As soon as they finished, all the white people in the restaurant who recognized the song applauded.

"Can you picture it now?" Jack asked. "The acoustic rock sound, close harmonies, good beat, and Jesus."

Jeff high-fived his brother. "Christian youth groups are going to eat us up, because we'll provide a safe outlet for them to rock out to."

"You wanna know what our duo name is?" asked Jack.

"Sure."

"Two for One," he said. "Do you get it?"

"Get what?"

"What our name means."

"Of course I get it. 'Two' stands for you and your brother. And I assume 'One' stands for God."

"That's it. I'm glad you get it. I was afraid it was too obscure. But check this out—we're not gonna spell out the word *for*. We're gonna use the number 4 instead."

"Oh, really?" I said. "That's clever. Numbers are really in right now."

"Yeah, I think it'll look pretty hot on our CD cover, don't you?"

I was about to confess that I thought the band name was awful, but before I gathered the courage to offer my opinion, Jack reached into a duffel bag and pulled out a black T-shirt with a brown cross down the middle. Written above the cross in a graffiti font were the words "Two4One."

"Here, this is for you." Jack tossed the shirt across the table at me. "Now you're an official Two4One groupie."

I thought about asking if God's calling for them had come with a box of instant T-shirts, but I didn't want to offend my famous friends. Like all famous people, I assumed that Jack and Jeff would soon have coattails for someone like me to ride.

The odd thing about Christians pursuing fame is that they do it while pretending not to be interested in fame. Their goal, most say, is not to bring fame and fortune to themselves. Their only interest is to make Jesus known. But in the process of making Jesus better known than he already is, a lot of Christian musicians find fame and fortune for themselves too. Jack and Jeff called that "reaping God's reward."

"It's not about us, Matthew," Jack told me multiple times. "Jeff and I desire only to glorify God with our music and live shows."

Four months after meeting the Gladstone Family, Jack asked if I wanted to go with him and Jeff to Gospel Music Week in Nashville. He plopped down a four-color brochure from the Gospel Music Association. Inside, pictures of Amy Grant, Sandi Patty, Michael W. Smith, and Petra sat next to detailed information about classes and seminars that musically gifted Christians could take to learn how to make it big in Christian music. As I salivated over all that Gospel Music Week offered, my mind wandered onto the conversation I'd had with Kathy. I pushed it out of my head and told Jack I would go.

On the drive to Nashville, Jack, Jeff, and I detoured through West Virginia. Poppa Gladstone was preaching a tent revival on the grounds of a church outside Huntington and wanted his boys to sing. I didn't mind the side trip, as it would be my first opportunity to see firsthand how famous Jack, Jeff, and Poppa really were.

Pulling into the parking lot of a Baptist church, Jack pointed at the yellow tent. "Looks like Daddy's already here."

Jeff nodded but didn't say anything.

The three of us got out of the car. "Hey, Daddy!" Jack yelled.

I looked up to see a man waddling toward us and waving. About five feet four in both height and width, Poppa Gladstone was by far the unhealthiest person I had ever seen in person. As he wobbled closer, I couldn't decide what part of him to look at. I felt guilty for staring, but Poppa's body offered so many viewing options: four chins, three plateaus of belly fat, and earlobes that dangled against the collar of his shirt when he turned his head. Then he spoke.

"You must be the Matthew I keep hearing about."

Far bigger and more captivating than the size of Poppa's body was his monstrosity of a voice. Never before had I heard my name spoken with such authority and power. The way Poppa said my name, it was like hearing "Matthew" bellowed from the belly of a humpback whale.

"That's me," I said, shaking his hand.

"Well, boys," said Mr. Gladstone, "they're expecting most of the town to come to the revival tonight."

Jack's and Jeff's faces lit up. "Good," said Jeff. "We got T-shirts to sell."

That evening when the Christian rock duo Two4One walked on stage to perform their five songs, people occupied exactly twenty-six of the five hundred folding chairs. Counting me. By the time Poppa Gladstone approached the pulpit, a family of three had decided to go home.

I thought, *Billy Graham must not be very popular in this part of West Virginia.*

Jack and Jeff didn't feel too famous after that gig, and much to my disappointment, neither did I.

The next day Two4One spent the first part of the drive to Nashville offering a list of excuses as to why the attendance was so sparse at their father's event. "That's the lowest it's ever been," Jeff said in disbelief. They placed most of the blame on the church's failure to advertise, which I thought was unfair.

"Well, thank goodness it's all about Jesus and not how famous your father is in West Virginia," I blurted out from the backseat. Then I just stared out the window and we sat in silence. I felt sort of proud of myself for speaking up. Twenty-four hours prior, I wouldn't have felt comfortable using such sarcasm around them, but after seeing how "famous" they were in West Virginia, and remembering the countless times they bragged about their father's popularity, I no longer feared losing Jack and Jeff's friendship. I still wanted to be their friends, but I didn't feel as controlled by it.

When Nashville's skyline peeked over the horizon of Interstate 65, my gut bubbled with nervous excitement. Jack looked at me in the backseat.

"For the record," he said, "we do want our music career to be all about Jesus, but that's hard sometimes. We get caught up in the stuff that doesn't matter."

"It's hard for all of us," I said. "Not just you two."

Jeff pulled the car into the parking garage of Nashville's downtown Stouffer Hotel. As we walked across the street to the hotel's lower-level entrance, I saw, hanging above the gold doors, a tractor trailer–sized sign promoting 4Him, a Christian quartet like New Kids on the Block without the sexy dance routines and the headbands. I stared at the massive banner, wondering why Jesus wasn't anywhere on it—just the four band members.

I walked into the hotel lobby, and as I looked around, I suddenly felt like I had died and gone to a type of heaven where only pretty and talented people mingled, hugged, and pretended to be interested in each other. I wasn't sure I belonged there, but I was definitely interested in signing up.

I ventured a few steps further, but was stopped by the hustle and bustle of the crowded lobby. Everywhere I looked, beautiful banners promoted beautiful Christians with beautiful voices. The people seemed so friendly too. Many of them smiled in my direction. A couple of them waved. I didn't know who any of them were, but I felt obligated to wave and smile back like they were old friends.

I'd only been standing in the lobby for a moment, and already people had handed me free music. Most of it looked like music that included electric pianos, tambourines, and copious amounts of polyester, but still, the gesture was thoughtful.

Standing in that Christian music paradise, I felt like Dorothy in the scene from *The Wizard of Oz* when the Munchkins welcome her with song, dance, and lollipops.

I looked at Jack. My hand covered my mouth, in awe of the spectacle. "See?" I said. "This is what *all about Jesus* is supposed to feel like. Like a candy factory—heavenly and sickeningly sweet all at the same time."

I thought, *I want to make Jesus lollipops.*

Three weeks after our trip to Nashville, Jack called me to say good-bye. He and Jeff had decided to move away from Chestertown and back to West Virginia. I didn't see or hear from either of them after that.

I called Kathy.

"You were right about them," I said.

She grunted, "I heard. Are you okay?"

"I'm actually sort of glad they left. It's exhausting riding the coattails of people pretending to be famous. Besides, I move to Nashville in a couple of months anyway, and perhaps Jesus will make me rich and famous for singing about him."

"If that happens," said Kathy, "call me. You might need to be rediagnosed."

Bubble Boy

The first time I went to a movie theater was in 1993, at age nineteen. A late bloomer, I was a twelvish-looking nineteen, but things were looking up since I'd discovered that God had actually given me an Adam's apple.

Just three days after my parents dropped me off at Belmont University in Nashville to study music business, I let my new friends Nadine and Pam lure me into a dark theater. I felt both nervous and excited about sitting in front of a big screen to watch what my church called the "excrement of hell."

"The *excrement* of hell?" Nadine choked on what looked like a vase of margarita at a T.G.I. Friday's the moment I confessed I had never seen *E.T.* A senior in Belmont's music business program, Nadine was well respected on campus. She coughed a couple of times and exclaimed, "We're going to rent it! It's almost impossible for me to believe you haven't seen *E.T.*"

"Really?" I said. "Because I know lots of people who were afraid to see *E.T.*"

Our fear of the movie was Brother Phil's fault. In 1982 he was the children's pastor at IBBC. After the evening service one Sunday, he called a special *E. T.* meeting to inform parents of the danger that Holly-wood's rich Jews and gay men posed to Christianity. These types of gatherings were usually organized when our church leadership learned that a parent had allowed a child to sin and then failed to tell him or her to avoid bragging about it at Sunday school.

The *E. T.* meeting was scheduled because a Sunday school teacher witnessed a female church member walking out of a movie theater with her son. The teacher claimed the child wore a black T-shirt with a picture of E.T. on the front, which proved he not only watched the movie, he had premeditated it.

My mom attended Brother Phil's meeting and walked away inspired.

"Apparently," my mother said, crossing her arms, "E.T. is an alien with a glowing fingertip he sometimes uses to do magic. And at one point in the movie, he touches his fingertip against the fingertip of a young boy."

Mom paused and raised her eyebrows at Dad and me as if her point was self-explanatory.

"And?" my father prompted a moment later. "What's that mean, exactly?"

"Oh Virgil, doesn't the fingertip imagery sound familiar?"

"Not really."

Mom uncrossed her arms. "The movie is making fun of Jesus, Virgil. And they're portraying him as an extraterrestrial."

"They think Jesus is a Martian?" I asked.

Mom nodded. "Sort of. An extraterrestrial doesn't have to be from Mars, sweetie, just outer space."

I understood the concept of being an alien because, at that age, I wanted people to think I was one. My motivation was purely spiritual. The pastor at my church told us that normal people look at good Baptists who possess holy and undefiled bodies and think they're alienlike creatures from heaven. Even though a stranger had never come up to me and told me I reminded him of an alien, I felt that E.T. might have understood me.

The way Brother Phil connected the dots from E.T. to Jesus was by way of Michelangelo's painting of God and Adam almost touching each other's fingers on the ceiling of the Sistine Chapel. Even though the famous rendering was known around my church as little more than Catholic graffiti, it carried enough historical significance for Brother Phil to suggest that the pivotal scene where E.T. touched fingertips with the movie's curious young boy was a mockery of Jesus.

"That sounds far-fetched," my father said.

"Oh, I can believe it, Virgil." My mother arched her eyebrows. "It makes me wonder if we'd be better off locking our kids in one of the closets so they won't be influenced by all the filth in the world."

I took her observation as my cue to run outside and hide.

Under the festive stained-glass T.G.I. Friday's chandelier, Nadine's stare began making me feel uncomfortable.

"Why are you so concerned about whether or not I watch E.T.?" I asked.

"Because you're a music business major, that's why."

"What does that have to do with anything?"

"Music business majors can't be oblivious to popular culture, Matthew," she said. "We have to learn from it—the good and the bad."

As a born-again Baptist, one that had only recently become comfortable with beats and bass lines, her ideas were hard to understand. I had hoped to ignore the world's bad music and just learn from Amy Grant's good kind.

Nadine said that was unacceptable. "But don't worry, Matthew," she told me. "You're in good hands. I'll introduce you to everything you missed out on."

Nadine kept looking at me like she was a PETA representative and I was a puppy being chased by Cruella De Vil. She planned to save me. Pam, Nadine's codependent and slightly neurotic roommate, was only there because she didn't have anything better to do on a Thursday evening.

Halfway through dinner Nadine put her elbows on the table and cupped her face. "So tell me this, Matthew. Did the people at your church really use the word *excrement* when referring to movies? That's an odd way to describe a movie."

"Well," I said, "people didn't always use that exact word. Some people called it dung or manure or caca."

"Wow, that's *very* odd," said Pam, turning to look at Nadine.

It wasn't odd to me, not in the least. That was how we described anything manufactured by the devil—movies, television shows, paperback novels with swooning women on the covers, and music. Members of my church hated music most of all. It was considered more dangerous than Satan's other forms of pop-cultural waste because it was everywhere. Accidentally stepping in Satan's movies or books rarely happened to good Baptists who resisted the temptation of basic cable or Waldenbooks, but stepping on music could happen almost anywhere—in grocery stores, public restrooms, bus stations, or at the community pool when sinners brought their boom boxes along with their towels.

"They called it *caca*?" Nadine plopped her head down on the table for dramatic effect. "Are you kidding? That's even stranger than *excrement*."

Pam laughed. "That's definitely strange. Who uses the word *caca*?"

"Mexicans do," I said, reaching for my glass of nonalcoholic sweet tea and leaning against the back of my chair. "And a large portion of South America."

"And apparently Baptists." Pam smiled at Nadine, hoping for approval.

I put my drink down and sighed. I don't know why I expected Nadine and Pam to understand my Christian faith; they were Lutherans, which as far as I was concerned meant they had more in common with the Dalai Lama than they did a Baptist. I wasn't an expert on the different denominations of Christianity, but I knew the basics about Lutheranism because I took a special six-week Sunday school class on false doctrines that my church offered. The teacher told us that today's Lutherans only went to church because it was fashionably correct to do so. He told us that their religious practices showed little resemblance to Martin Luther, their namesake.

"That man reeked of Calvinism," the teacher said, "but he didn't pussyfoot around the lies of Catholicism. He did something. If Luther knew what his followers were up to today, he'd have ninety-five *different* theses to nail onto a church door somewhere."

Pam looked like a Lutheran.

Lutheran women sometimes shopped at the Christian bookstore I worked at on weekends and after school. The ones who frequented

Chestertown's Mustard Seed bookshop wore their hair short and spiky like elves. Most of them wore clothes that looked like they'd come from the young boys' section at the Gap. Lutheran women also didn't like to hide their pale complexions underneath a little makeup or moisturizer. Pam had all those symptoms. Plus, she drove a Volvo with a vegetarian sticker on the bumper.

But Nadine looked different. Her clothes sported fancy European labels, and she smelled like her neck and wrists had been dabbed with potent exotic flowers. Nadine liked her colors bright, her music loud, and her margaritas green and blended. People stared when Nadine walked into the room, not because she was loud or obnoxious or seeking attention, but because they couldn't help it. Unlike the Lutheran women who didn't seem to like cosmetics, scarves, or bras, Nadine proudly called herself a "lipstick Lutheran."

Pam curled her upper lip. "I have a question, Matthew—did anybody just use the word *poop*? Why speak Spanish when you could just say it in English?"

"Because we weren't allowed to say that word unless referring to real poop."

Pam gasped. "Please tell me you're kidding."

"I'm not kidding."

"Wait, what if you had been born in Mexico—would you have been allowed to say caca?"

Pam thought she was being smart, but her question was nothing I hadn't heard before. My friends and I discussed these kinds of things all the time. Though we were astute in Baptist theology, we wondered if some sins were contingent on a person's geography.

For example, we heard rumors that Baptists in France were

allowed to go to topless beaches and drink chardonnay without keeping it a secret from the rest of their congregations. This always
intrigued us, since most of us kept our vacations to beaches where
women wore bathing suits a secret. It didn't matter what the women
looked like either. They could be hot like Lynda Carter or have a *great
personality* like Nell Carter—seeing any of them in bathing suits, even
the kind that came with frilly skirts that covered a woman's backside,
was sinful. We envied French Baptists. They seemed to worship a God
we didn't know.

I didn't know whether or not Baptists in Mexico were allowed to say
the word *caca,* so I told Pam she would have to ask a Mexican Baptist.

Nadine grinned at Pam. "He's a regular Beaver Cleaver, isn't he?"

Eyebrows arched, Pam said, "You know who Matthew reminds
me of? That seventies TV movie about the sick kid who was allergic
to being outside, so he had to live inside a clear plastic bubble."

"Oh my God, you're a freakin' genius, Pam." Nadine's voice was
loud enough that people began to stare. "*The Boy in the Plastic Bubble!* That's a perfect analogy." Nadine looked across the table at me.
"*Please,* Matthew, can we call you 'The Boy in the Plastic Bubble'?
Please let us." Then, as if she thought it sweetened her request, she
added, "John Travolta played the boy. And he was cute back then."

I nodded.

For the rest of the evening, Nadine and Pam referred to me as
Bubble Boy.

They also decided to take me to see my first movie at a theater,
which made me anxious. I took a long pull of my sweet tea.

When I arrived at Belmont, I wasn't accustomed to having Christian friends who could be bad influences on me without my parents

getting in the way. And in all my nineteen years, Mom and Dad always got in the way.

The freedom of going away to college excited me, but I hadn't spent much time thinking about how I would use it. I wasn't the kind of kid who, since learning of the existence of college in sixth grade, schemed about the various ways I wanted to "sin" when I got there. The kids from my church and Christian school who did make those kinds of plans never made it to college. Both of them had started breast-feeding by the eleventh grade and were currently studying for their GEDs.

My "evil" muscle was lazy and out of shape, honestly, so I didn't leave home with a strategy for sin. That was far too proactive for me. If I sowed my oats while at Belmont, a trusted companion would have to lead the way. Not so they could protect me from anything terrible, but so I would have somebody to blame if the "dung" hit the fan or managed to make its way back to my parents.

But I feared that Nadine was right, that my innocence might cripple my chances of "making it" in Nashville.

On the following Tuesday, Nadine walked into Music Business History, a required course for any music business major and the only class she and I took together, and sat at the desk behind me. The first thing she asked was when I was going with her and Pam to see a movie.

Before I had a chance to answer, Professor Watson walked into the classroom. A tall man with a long, egg-shaped face and an impressive mustache, Professor Watson looked as though God had thoughtfully considered making him a walrus.

Nadine told me Professor Watson was a disgruntled songwriter who became a teacher so he could eat. She also informed me that he was one of Belmont's *non-Christian* professors. Nadine thought that Belmont's roots in the Southern Baptist Convention became shallower every year. Professor Watson was proof.

As an introduction to the first day of class, Professor Watson told us a story.

"My life changed on a fall day in 1965," he said. "What happened that day might be the one and only reason I am here teaching this class. I was lying on the hood of my buddy's Mercury Monterey, smoking a cigarette I'd rolled myself. On Fridays after school, a bunch of my friends and I hung out in the empty parking lot behind the Piggly Wiggly. That was a special day because I was wearing my brand-new Native Indian–styled leather coat my parents bought me for my birthday. It felt like suede but wasn't quite as soft. I loved that coat. The color was camel. Those coats were hard to come by in Huntsville, but I found a catalog for a mom-and-pop manufacturer in Butte, Montana. You'd probably be surprised what you can get in Native Indian Leather."

Professor Watson had only been talking for a minute or two and already I assumed he was an unmarried man with a transistor radio in his bedroom.

"As I lounged there, smoking a good cigarette, my friend turned on the car radio." Professor Watson's eyes gleamed, and he walked over to the CD player sitting on the table next to his podium. "And for the first time, my friends, I heard this song. My life hasn't been the same since."

He pushed Play. Recognizing the song, the guy on the front row wearing a PUMA T-shirt and prescription eyewear that turned into sunglasses in bright conditions began bopping his head.

"This is Dylan's 'Like a Rolling Stone,'" he said. "I love this song. Dylan's a frickin' genius."

Most of the members of the class nodded in agreement, and one by one, their nodding transformed into bopping. I imagined their eyes swirling, sometimes rolling to the back of their heads. Obviously, they liked what they heard. Several hooted and pumped their fists in the air when the first harmonica solo started. One of my classmates closed his eyes and began moving his fists like he was beating a drum set that hovered above his desk. Another sitting in the back row patted his hand over his heart. And a girl with pink hair, who sat close enough to me that I could smell what kind of shampoo she used, confessed her willingness to have Dylan's love child. The scene that broke out in my classroom seemed drug-induced. I always imagined a similar scene would occur at a pastors' convention if Ronald Reagan keynoted.

When the song finished, Professor Watson grinned. "I'm happy to know I have a class full of Dylan fans. Now you understand why hearing that song changed my life."

Everyone in the class except me nodded their heads like zombies, hanging on his every word.

"I would think that *loving* Dylan would be a music business requirement," said the pink-haired girl. "I mean, he revolutionized not only the music scene, but also politics, art, and in a way, our entire American culture."

She sounded like the kind of person my father called "a godforsaken hippie."

"You're exactly right," Professor Watson said. "That's why we study the history of how our industry works, because the artists who make music affect much more than just music. Real artists affect our lives."

I raised my hand.

As soon as I did, Nadine poked my back. "What are you doing? Put your hand down. I'm serious, put your hand down."

She was whispering, so by the time I realized she was serious, Professor Watson had pointed at me. "Yes?"

"Hello, Professor Watson," I said, hearing what sounded like Nadine's head plunking against her desk.

"What's your name?" asked Professor Watson.

"Matthew Turner."

"What's your question, Matthew?"

"Should I know who Dylan is?"

The room's commotion screeched to a halt. Every eyeball focused on me.

"Yes. You should know who Dylan is."

"Okay," I said, "I'll see about getting his CDs. But can I ask you another question?"

He nodded.

"Why did that song change your life?"

His jaw fell open, but he didn't say anything, so I figured he wanted me to explain my question further.

"It just isn't *that* good of a song. The melody does nothing but repeat itself over and over again, and his singing voice is nasal and seemingly incapable of staying on pitch. I'm not sure the song has a pitch to stay on. To be honest I'm not sure how this Dylan guy made a career in the music industry."

As everyone in the class broke into laughter, I once again heard Nadine's head hit her desk. She whispered, "*Why* did you just ask that? Don't hate me if I pretend not to know you for the next few minutes."

I was getting ready to respond to Nadine's question when the pink-haired girl turned around and frowned at me. Actually, her facial expression might have been more of a scowl or a death glare or a sign of the end times. Whatever it was, it scared me.

Obviously, she was angry with me for taking her lord's name in vain and was about to reveal unto me her wrath. As I watched her mouth open, expecting to see vampire fangs, she spoke.

"I'm gonna close my eyes, and when I open them, you better be on your knees asking the great Bob Dylan for forgiveness."

"Are you insane?" I said. "I only bow down to Jesus, and this Dylan guy can't even sing, so I know he's not Jesus."

"He might not be Jesus, but he's darn close!" Pink-haired girl's nostrils engorged, making her look like a Pekingese. I waited for her to growl at me, or at the very least yap a few times.

Professor Watson's voice interrupted the commotion. He looked at me and said, "There's somebody like you in every one of my classes, Matthew. I take it you're here to make it in the *Christian* music industry, am I right?"

"Yes sir."

"Good luck passing my class," he said. Then he smiled. Not a kind smile—a smile that reeked of sarcasm and loathing. He didn't bother to answer my questions about Bob Dylan.

After class Nadine informed me that she thought Professor Watson pretty much hated me and that I would have to work really hard to pass his class.

"This is why you can't shy away from listening to music and watching movies," she said.

She offered to have her mom and dad send her their Time Life music collections so I could catch up on the music I'd never heard.

"I know they have the best of the sixties and seventies." Nadine laughed. "We were Lutherans, so it wasn't against our Christianity to have monthly subscriptions to caca. It just came in the mail every month, and then we had seven days to decide whether we wanted to keep it. We usually did."

I sighed.

"What's wrong?" asked Nadine.

"Nothing. Just not excited about having to become familiar with four decades of crap."

"Yeah, it won't be easy. But at least Time Life presents the best of the best crap."

That Friday evening Nadine and Pam took me to Fountain Square's Carmike 14. As Nadine pulled the car into the parking lot, she glanced at my face in her rearview mirror.

"Stop looking so frightened, Matthew."

"I'm not scared. Just quiet, that's all."

"This is going to be fun." She turned to Pam. "I've never watched somebody lose their movie-theater virginity before. In high school my friend and I thought we saw somebody lose her actual virginity in a movie theater, but that's different. You know, messier."

As the three of us walked across the parking lot toward the theater's ticket counter, I did feel like I was about to lose something. I felt like I was having an out-of-body experience, like I was taking a vacation away from life as I knew it.

I thought about my sister Kelley. She'd gone to a movie theater when she was nineteen. The movie didn't seem to affect her behavior until my mother found out about it.

Mom's reaction caused a shift in my town's barometric pressure. They yelled and screamed at each other for an hour, and then Kelley stormed out the front door, got into her station wagon, and peeled out of the driveway. Mom fled to her bedroom and threw herself onto her bed. Her sobbing was laced with pain, like she had lost something she could never get back. Only eleven, I sat on my bedroom floor and cried. At that moment I wasn't sure I would ever see Kelley again, and I wasn't convinced my mother wanted to.

For as long as I could remember, I had lived a separate existence from normal people. I don't believe I comprehended to what extent my life was different from the lives of other people my age, but I wasn't naive to how odd and detached we were. Sure, my parents installed a chastity belt around my brain to keep out unwanted predators like Pee-wee Herman and the anti-God propagandist who wrote 1984, but I wasn't ignorant. I knew my family was different. We liked being different.

Why wouldn't God find pleasure in my holy brown-nosing? Most of the people at my church did. As far as I knew, the faith I lived was built on nothing less than the state of my own righteousness.

I wanted to go to the theater. But I did fear that when the movie was over, I'd struggle to envision God looking at me with the same delight as he did before.

At my church my sins weren't so much saved by grace. They were taunted by it.

A few minutes into the movie, I laughed. Then I laughed again.

The devil's poop was funny.

When we walked out of the theater, I did feel a little different. At the time, I wasn't sure if it was God's doing or because I'd just sat through 104 minutes of *Robin Hood*…

Men in Tights.

Home

For a long time I separated the Christians who attended Belmont University into two different groups: those who enjoyed gathering in small circles for Bible reading and prayer, and those whose idea of "Jesus time" was ducking behind a Dumpster so they could smoke "socially" alone.

Then there was my friend Josiah, the only person I knew who managed to mingle in both groups. Sometimes when he could convince his circle of friends to hold hands adjacent to one of Belmont's six Dumpsters, he participated in both groups at the same time. Whenever one of his Christian friends questioned his nicotine habit, Josiah always said the same thing.

"I used to be Amish, all right? Amish! Do you know what it was like being raised Amish? The only difference between being Amish and being dead is that my coffin was pulled by a horse and dropped me off at Wal-Mart on Saturday morning."

Josiah was the only passive-aggressive former Amish person I'd ever met. In college he tried really hard to get back at his parents for making him Amish. He did this by taking up smoking and becoming a Calvinist.

Josiah and I met on my first day at Belmont. My parents, my sister Elisabeth, and I had just arrived in Nashville, and the four of us had just finished circling a building, trying to determine if it contained my dorm room.

"Dad, this can't be it," I said.

My father pulled the car over and snatched the college map out of my fingers. "I'm pretty sure this is right, Buck."

"You must have made a wrong turn somewhere, Dad."

"Buck, I'm tellin' ya, we're right in front of your dorm. It's that middle one, right there."

Dad pointed at a three-story brick building on top of a small hill. Pembroke Hall looked nothing like it did in the pictures. The brochure said it possessed a "historic grandeur," so I knew it wouldn't be a new building. What the brochure didn't say was that Pembroke appeared old enough to have been built by Confederates.

The pictures made Pembroke seem warm and inviting. One featured a group of seven guys sitting on the back steps, laughing, eating pizza, and enjoying the guitar skills of the one Asian guy in the picture. Those steps looked like the perfect location for lounging, studying, or gathering with a racially diverse group of friends for a game of Uno or Bible trivia.

In person, the windows were cracked, with paint chipping off the sills; some bricks looked loose, and four of the ten air-conditioning units hanging out of the first-floor windows were supported by two-by-fours and plywood. It didn't look warm and inviting. It looked like the front yard on the set of *Sanford and Son*.

I sighed.

"Doesn't look the same as it does in the pictures, huh?" I said this only because I knew Dad, Mom, and Elisabeth were already thinking it. Nobody said anything. I looked at Elisabeth, hoping she'd offer something positive.

Her eyes searched the building, and she leaned over the front seat to look at the picture in the brochure. "That's *not* the same building. It's not. The actual building looks *nothing* like that. The picture makes you think you're going to live in Colonial Williamsburg. This place looks like a homeless shelter."

My mother sat in the front passenger seat, nodding. "I was thinking the same thing, Lis." Mom spun around to face me. "Lis is right— your dorm does look like a homeless shelter. Oh, and *look*..."

Leaning her head sideways, Mom raised her eyebrows, indicating Elisabeth and I should look out the passenger window. Walking toward us was a young man with long brown hair, a pale complexion, and a bushy beard. Elisabeth hopped to the center of the backseat for a better look.

"Do you think that's a homeless man?" she asked.

"He *is* carrying a guitar," my mother said, checking "guitar carrier" off her mental list of homeless prerequisites. "Lots of homeless people play instruments. That's how they make money."

My father glanced at the man. "Oh, I doubt he's homeless, but I'll admit he's a rough-looking character." Dad turned toward me. "Buck, what kind of college is Belmont?"

"He stopped walking!" announced Elisabeth. The four of us watched the man like he might break into a chorus of "His Banner Over Me Is Love" in hopes of winning a percentage of our tithes and offerings. "What do you think he's going to do?"

A few yards away from our car, the man set his guitar case down on the sidewalk and began fumbling through his backpack. Elisabeth commented that if he showered and shaved, she thought he could be nice looking and even potentially resemble Jesus. Mom disagreed.

"I think he's going to play a song." Elisabeth made no effort to hide her curiosity. "Yep, he's going to play something. He's opening his guitar case."

"This is a music school," I said. "That would make sense."

Elisabeth rolled her eyes. "Lock the doors, Dad."

"Oh, come on. He's not going to hurt us with his guitar," I said.

"He could have something in his book bag," said my mother in her only *half*-joking tone. "I have a hard time trusting any adult who carries a book bag. I've watched too many reruns of *L.A. Law.* The criminals on that show always carry book bags."

"I carry a book bag, Mom," I said.

The man pulled out a cigarette and lighter, and a couple of moments later, he puffed while he strummed the guitar.

"I thought Belmont was a *Christian* college." Elisabeth had never witnessed somebody partake in tobacco products while standing on God's property. "He's smoking."

My father deemed it safe to get out of the car. Elisabeth opened her door and waved her hand in front of her face, just in case nicotine floated in the air. Dad unlocked the car's trunk, and we started unloading suitcases and boxes full of clothes, sheets and towels, and CDs. The "homeless" man smashed his cigarette on the cement.

"Dad," whispered Elisabeth, "I think he's going to ask you for money."

The bearded guy extended a hand toward me. "Hey, I'm Josiah."

Dad and I shook his hand. Mom and Elisabeth waved from a safe distance.

"I'm one of the volunteers who help new students move in. Would you like some help?"

As Elisabeth and I dragged suitcases up the stairs to Pembroke's second floor, I whispered, "See? He's not homeless."

She whispered back, "Maybe not. But if his bad guitar playing is any indication, there's still a chance that he could end up that way."

Josiah moved to Nashville from Indiana because, like most of us, he dreamed of making music. Specifically, he wanted to write songs about how much he loved God and predestination. In 1993 believing in predestination was trendy among Christian musicians. Josiah loved it so much that he believed God predestined him to help Calvinism make a comeback.

"Don't laugh," he told people who poked fun at the idea. "It's going to be bigger than Meatloaf's comeback! America was founded by Calvinists. Without them, you might have been Eastern European."

Josiah and I didn't instantly become best friends after our first meeting; he was one of Belmont's artsy Christian musicians, and I was not. Unlike the other talented people Josiah palled around with, I still brushed my hair, my complexion wasn't ghostly, and my appearance never caused people to question, from a distance, whether I used deodorant. Nothing in my wardrobe was made out of flannel or that colorful burlaplike material popular among Hispanics and pot smokers. Plus, I couldn't play guitar, which for a believer at Belmont was like being Jewish and uncircumcised.

But the primary reason I didn't fit in with Josiah's group of friends was because I wasn't Presbyterian.

All of Belmont's artsy kids were Presbyterians, except for those whose artsiness was of a Broadway persuasion; then they were Pentecostal.

Most students didn't come to Belmont as Presbyterians. The majority were Southern Baptists. But if they wanted to be accepted as real singers, musicians, or songwriters, sooner or later they gave in to the peer pressure of Belmont's artsy community and began showing "Presbyterian" signs. They stopped brushing their hair and started wearing flannel shirts and black combat boots.

Before long, they started carrying around Puritan prayer books and could be seen reading *My Utmost for His Highest* between classes. At that point it wouldn't be long before they began writing songs about Jonathan Edwards and avoiding direct contact with the sun.

A Belmont student's conversion to Calvinism was complete when they started telling people they were born that way.

A couple of weeks into my first semester, as Josiah and I walked from the cafeteria to the men's dorms, Josiah asked if I'd found a church I liked yet.

"I'm still visiting around," I told him. "There're so many churches in Nashville. It's hard to tell the difference."

Josiah lit a cigarette. "Ah," he said, blowing smoke out of his nostrils. "I'm a Calvinist."

Josiah said "Calvinist" the same way Kurt Cobain said the word *marijuana* or Hillary Clinton said the words *health care*. I didn't know one thing about Calvinism, but I nodded like I did.

I was familiar with the word. That is, I'd heard it once. A few years before, my father mentioned it as we drove by the little church that met across the street from ours. The fifty-member congregation was falling apart for the fifth time in ten years. Dad seemed to think the church's problems had something to do with the pastor being a Calvinist. At the time, I figured it was his race or nationality or perhaps something like being a Texan.

"Yeah, my folks wouldn't be happy about my reformed beliefs." Josiah sucked on the end of his cigarette. "They'd probably think I fell off the deep end. But whatever. At some point you gotta stop caring."

He tossed his cigarette butt on the sidewalk in front of him and smashed it with his foot.

"So, any chance you're a Calvinist?"

When I didn't answer right away, Josiah stopped walking and slapped my back. "Wait. You're not Arminian, are you?"

I hesitated because I didn't know how to answer his question. *I'm just a Baptist,* I thought, but that wasn't one of the options.

"Uh, Matthew, you do know what I'm referring to, right? The two types of theologies?"

"They're theologies?"

"Yeah. You know, different ways of thinking about God."

"I've heard the word *Calvinist* before, but I'm not familiar with it. And I've never heard that other word."

"That's incredible," said Josiah. "I was raised *Amish,* and I learned about Calvinism and Arminianism."

"I was raised Baptist. I don't think we had an official theology. We were just Baptist-y."

As far as I knew, our church didn't have an official theology. Not unless you counted Baptist as its own thing. Sure, people studied biblical things, but nobody really studied *God* at my church. One of the deacons claimed to know everything about the Jewish faith, which he'd use to prove why Christianity was true. But that was it—there was no official statement.

Talking to Josiah made me feel dumb.

I didn't study God. I just memorized Scripture verses and practiced Bible trivia. I could have told you the names of the twelve sons of Jacob or offered you a biblically accurate play-by-play of the events that led up to King David sleeping with Bathsheba. I learned facts. I knew a thousand Bible verses by heart, but I couldn't explain why God's story was important to me, personally.

At least not without using hell as a starting point.

"Everybody has some sort of theology." Josiah tossed his book bag on the stairs in front of his dorm. "Even no theology is something. I mean, even atheists have a theology, in my opinion." He swung his head back and tossed his hair out of his face. "Why don't you come to church with me on Sunday and find out?"

"I don't know, man," I said. "I need to research this John Calvin guy before I jump into one of his churches."

"Matthew, my church is awesome. And hey, Amy Grant goes there."

"Amy Grant goes to your church?"

He smiled and nodded.

"Where and when should I meet you?"

"Eight thirty. Meet us right here."

Crammed inside a Toyota Corolla, five of us went to church that morning. Josiah drove while his girlfriend, Leah, sat in the passenger's seat with her hand on his leg. Her fingers kept tapping his thigh like it was a toy piano.

On either side of me in the backseat sat David and Ed, two bearded Calvinist friends of Josiah's and also his band mates. During his freshman year, Josiah had started a Christian rock band with what I thought was a rather cocky name: The 96th Thesis. Though I wasn't aware that Martin Luther was Calvinist, I did know that his ninety-five theses aided in changing European history. I hadn't yet heard the band's music, but Josiah described it as Pearl Jam meets Petra meets the Pilgrims.

Josiah and Leah seemed excited about my attending church with them. I was excited too, for two reasons: (1) I hoped going to their church would help my pursuit of being accepted in Belmont's artsy music clique, and (2) I felt kind of rebellious calling my mother the day before and telling her that I was planning to worship among Presbyterians.

"Amy Grant goes there," I said. "I might get to meet her."

"Great, Matthew." I heard her sigh. "But does God go there?"

"I think so. But wouldn't it be cool if I was able to get my Bible signed by the *real* Amy Grant?"

To Independent Fundamental Baptists, the Word of God was very holy, but it was also an autograph book. Any time we met famous preachers or evangelists, we would stand in line after their sermons and ask them to sign our Bibles. At one point I got tired of having only the autographs of male preachers, so I forged the signatures of Sandi Patty and Amy Grant into my Bible. I'd always wanted the opportunity to cross out their fake signatures and replace them with real ones.

In preparation for going to Christ Community Church, Nashville's well-known Presbyterian Church of America congregation, I went to Belmont's library and searched through the Calvinism section. I thought it would be a good idea to at least know something about the perspectives of Calvinists prior to hanging out with a group of them for four hours on Sunday.

Most of the books I found were a thousand pages long and written in size-eight font, but eventually I found and read a pamphlet called "The Nutshell of Calvinism." It didn't help much, leaving me with a lot more questions than answers.

God predestines people to heaven? He chooses people for hell?

As far as I was concerned, John Calvin made the grace of God sound like a hopeless mess. Hardly irresistible.

What I read in that pamphlet scared me. Which was saying something, considering my church burned Barbie dolls to ignite young imaginations on what hell might be like. But as spiritually unstable as the people in my church were sometimes, not one of them believed God was mean enough to *choose* who goes to hell. Reformed people seemed to reduce God to a moody, all-knowing, and all-powerful maître d'. Some folks were just automatically seated in the smoking section.

I wasn't sure why anybody would want to be Calvinist. Not voluntarily, anyway. Maybe if there was a bonus or some kind of incentive built into the program, but as far as I was concerned, the doctrine of depravity seemed to shoot any "Reformed benefits" to hell. What befuddled me more than anything was what artists—people who tell stories and dream and help the rest of us find light and hope in the ugliness of life—found appealing about Calvinism. I assumed there must be something about it that I didn't see, because at Belmont, the cool Christians, the ones who wore flip-flops, played acoustic guitars, and stole song ideas from U2 albums really seemed infatuated with John Calvin.

Leah certainly was. A singer-songwriter with a voice Josiah compared to the purity of Sarah McLachlan's, Leah obsessed about the teachings of Calvin.

"I think you're going to love Pastor Scotty's preaching, Matthew." Leah's personality was pretty as a daisy. Cute and thin and dressed like spring in a yellow skirt and blouse, Leah was an artsy guy's dream. Not perfect looking, but honest and unadulterated, and she smelled good. Most impressive was her blond hair; twisted and interlaced and gathered into a braid in the back, her locks looked like they'd been woven together with the precision of a basket maker.

"Scotty's amazing," said Leah, "and so down to earth. The man wears sandals." She tapped Josiah's thigh. "Isn't that right, hon? Doesn't he wear sandals almost every Sunday?"

"Yeah, man," he said, "and they are *sweet.* You can tell he gets the expensive kind. I'd do almost anything for a pair."

Josiah and Leah looked at each other and giggled, and then Leah glanced back at me.

"Josiah *loves* Scotty's sandals," she said.

It was obvious the two of them had previously discussed Josiah's desire to have a pair of Pastor Scotty's sandals. I watched Leah squeeze Josiah's hand. It was a long and thoughtful squeeze, as though she was letting him know he shouldn't worry, she was already conspiring to infiltrate Pastor Scotty's closet.

Pastor Scotty's footwear was famous around Belmont. How he

dressed his feet was his trademark, the way he told regular people he was just a regular guy. Wearing a pair of nice leather thongs seemed to tell those who loved him, "Hey, I'm just like you. I take my kids to soccer practice on Tuesday and Thursday afternoons."

It seemed odd that a pastor would feel comfortable enough to stand in front of his church with his toes hanging out, but I was excited to see Pastor Scotty's sandals. I'd never witnessed God's man walk across a church stage without socks—unless he was playing Jesus in an Easter cantata. Considering how uptight the pastor at my old church was, I was really interested in seeing how somebody with such an angry and carte blanche theology could be so casual and laid back.

"Anyway," said Leah, "I think you'll enjoy the service. I've been in church all my life, and I have never learned more about God from anybody than from Scotty."

"That's because your church's theology was all wrong."

Ed's voice startled me. Not because he was loud, but because he hadn't said a word since we'd gotten into the car, and the first thing he said came across as condescending.

Leah's smile diminished as she turned to look out her window.

"Let's face it, Leah, the reason you get so much out of Scotty's preaching is because it comes from a completely different perspective than the church you grew up in."

When she didn't respond, Ed scooted forward in his seat, forcing me to lean back. "Well, am I right? Don't you think that's it, that you're now studying truth? When you weren't before?"

I expected Leah to put Ed in his rightful place—back against the seat and mouth zipped shut. Or that Josiah would chime in and support Leah. But neither of them said anything. The longer I watched

Ed wait for Leah or Josiah to accept his spiritual duel, the more frustrated I became.

I looked over at David, the other fellow churchgoer, but he didn't look back. His round, hairy face hadn't turned from the window since we got in the car, and he appeared unaware of his surroundings. Either that or he was used to Ed sparring during Sunday-morning drives to church.

When it was obvious nobody was going to say something, I cleared my throat.

"You might have a point, Ed," I said carefully. "A new theology can certainly make somebody feel alive or refreshed. But you shouldn't talk to Leah like that."

"It's not simply a new theology," he said. "It's a *true* one. There's a difference."

"Right, Ed. I understand, but it doesn't mean that everything Leah experienced before going to this church wasn't valuable or meaningful to her. It was just different."

"You're missing my point: it was also *not* the truth. At least not God's truth."

Our exchange of words continued from mile marker 74 to mile marker 65.

"As far as I'm concerned, if you don't know truth, Matthew, then you don't know God."

Blood rushed up the back of my neck and into my head. My skull began to pound.

Ed flipped through his New American Standard Bible, which I later learned was the Calvinist's translation of choice because it contained the least emotional phrasing. I wasn't sure what he was looking up, but I clasped my hands together as I thought about what my mother said when I argued with her about God: "You wear me out, Matthew."

I changed the subject. Sort of.

"You're a bass player, aren't you, Ed?"

He looked at me. "What does that have to do with anything?"

"Because you act like a bass player."

"I act like a bass player?"

I shared with them my theory about bass players. I didn't know a lot of popular music, but the bands I did listen to I'd studied intently. I developed a theory about bass players, that most of them were hiding some sort of unresolved anger. The crowd often forgets about the bass player. The lead singer is center stage, the guitar player gets to solo, and the drummer is the person everybody wishes they could be, but the bass player doesn't seem that interesting to watch. But he or she is the unflashy glue that keeps a band together. Without that steady talent, none of the other band members would sound nearly as good. Required to be the rock of the group, without the adulation—that might give anyone the emotional stability of a fourth-grade girl.

To the best of my ability, I said that in the friendliest tone possible, never letting the grin leave my face.

Josiah started laughing. "Dude," he said to Ed, "he nailed you."

I looked at Ed. His lips shook with anger and embarrassment.

In truth, the only reason I "nailed" Ed was because I was like him in a lot of ways. I couldn't play the bass guitar, but I had a lot of anger and emotion hiding inside me. Since high school, I'd been known as the guy who went unnoticed, the type of person people often considered a good "background" friend. I was that somebody who got invited to a party so the room would be full, not because people thought I was interesting or would make their social event more exciting or funny.

Three weeks before leaving for college, I started writing a song called "Independence Day." The lyrics revealed my frustration. The first verse started with these words:

It's Independence Day, but I am locked in chains
I'd love to wave a flag around, but instead I feel insane

The first thing I did when I walked into Christ Community Church was look for Amy Grant. Leah helped me search by pretending she needed to use the bathroom to see if Amy was in there. I walked by the nursery and the Sunday school classrooms but didn't see her anywhere. Josiah said she was probably on tour or went to a different service.

We walked into Christ Community's auditorium. The sanctuary smelled like a forest of pine trees. Its hardwood floors and solid wood beams made it feel warm, like a log cabin. Pastor Scotty was just like Leah described him. On that morning he wore a plaid shirt with khaki pants and a pair of his trademark sandals. What surprised me was how full of passion and wonder for God Pastor Scotty seemed. He wasn't at all like I anticipated. He didn't yell or scream like the fundamentalist preachers I was familiar with, nor did he mention anything about the chances that God had chosen certain members of his congregation to burn in hell. I had expected him to point people out, let them plan accordingly.

He preached about how much God loved King David, and how King David pursued dwelling in the house of the Lord. "Each of us was created to live in God's house," he told us. "Every one of us has a place at his table. It's an open invitation to sit and dine with our Creator."

I was confused, mostly because Pastor Scotty's sermon sounded nothing like what I'd read in "The Nutshell of Calvinism." He didn't talk about five points or tulips. He seemed nothing like a Puritan. Maybe it was his sandals that made him seem kind and approachable.

On the ride home, David sat on the hump in the backseat so Ed wouldn't have to sit next to me. I stared out the window for most of the trip back to campus, thinking about Pastor Scotty's words about God's house, and how, at that moment, I felt sort of homeless.

Josiah and I became good friends because I started going to church with him and Leah on Sundays. Our conversations before and after the service mostly revolved around debating and arguing theology. He seemed convinced I was a born-again Calvinist and just didn't know it.

When his band began putting together songs for an EP, I agreed to write a lyric for a melody he was working on. We both thought the song was pretty, but it didn't make it on the record because a couple of the other band members didn't think it meshed with their theology.

I dabbled in Calvinism enough to become accepted by Belmont's artsy Christians. I'm not sure I ever truly understood the people in that group, but I learned how to look like I did. I bought a pair of combat boots and a selection of flannel shirts, and for special occasions, I got a deal on a ruffled, white, button-down long-sleeved shirt at a secondhand store downtown. My friends said it made me look like a gay pirate, but I didn't care. When I wore that shirt, I felt dark, artistic, and because it brought me attention, visible.

By the time I finished the first semester of my sophomore year at

Belmont, I'd become Presbyterian enough to dye my hair black and purchase a New American Standard Bible. I even started looking for opportunities to use words like *covenant, depravity,* and *Martin Luther* in everyday conversations.

Most people thought I was a fully-fledged Calvinist when I began carrying around a book of Puritan prayers and sayings.

But I wasn't a full-on Calvinist. At the most, I believed three and a half of the five points to be true. The only time I became a five-point Calvinist was when I went home to Chestertown and my father and I felt like arguing about God's sovereignty. Those arguments brought out the worst in both of us. Dad turned into the stubborn legalist who had no patience for ideas that differed from his, and I turned into the punk know-it-all son with a religious ax to grind.

I liked being Calvinist because it made me feel controversial and edgy to believe something different than what my parents believed. On those trips home, I felt like I was experiencing my own little Protestant Reformation, hammering various disagreements I had with my past into my parents' faces.

I think that's why people like Josiah and me sometimes turned into Calvinists. We could be passive-aggressive toward our parents and our past lives without being considered unchristian. Reformed doctrine offered a different way to think about God. And sometimes *different,* even when it really isn't that different, is all we need to make us feel alive, creative, and in control of our own destiny.

One of Us

During college my friend Shawn was incredibly sensitive to onions, dairy, and the Holy Spirit. But unlike his allergies to food, Shawn bragged about his susceptibility to God's earthly essence. When he and I met, one of the first things he told me was that the Holy Spirit had led him to Belmont to become a church music major.

I wasn't surprised, considering God's spirit called me to go to Belmont too. Belmont was a Christian school, so lots of us attended because the Holy Spirit told us to. It was such a common occurrence that sometimes I wondered if the Holy Ghost worked part-time in Belmont's admissions office.

The way I talked about God's Spirit changed during college, mostly because some people thought I sounded mentally handicapped when I shared the things I believed the Holy Spirit told me to do or, as was often the case, not do.

God's Spirit told me to say hello to strangers and leave small pamphlets of information about Jesus on tables for waiters and waitresses or at urinals for strangers with full bladders and empty souls. Once, he told me to stop shopping at Structure and the Gap because of their sexy advertising campaigns. I stopped hanging out with certain friends because of the Holy Spirit's voice in my head, and on two occasions, he told me it was okay to break a girl's heart. Sadly, it was the same girl both times.

But I grew weary of hearing the still, small voice in my head, partly because it was the loudest, most obnoxious still, small voice I'd ever heard, but mostly because I started wondering if it was really God's voice or simply my own. I also got tired of people, mostly Christian people, calling me a freak for talking about the Holy Spirit like I was wearing a two-way hearing aid and in constant communication with heaven.

Unlike my childhood, when God and I talked incessantly and about most anything, the conversations began dwindling by my second year at Belmont. Consequently, I started doubting other people when they talked about hearing the Holy Spirit's voice all the time. Not every time. Most of my friends only mentioned the third member of the Trinity around certain holidays, like Easter and Halloween, or on the rare occasion when God made his opinions about their lives abundantly clear.

But my friend Shawn was different. He was a charismatic Baptist, which sounded like an oxymoron to me. Shawn's interactions with the Holy Spirit stood out because of how expressive he was about them and how often they occurred. For instance, Shawn's story about how he ended up in Belmont's church music program was more peculiar than most. He made it seem epic in a biblical way, as if a fiery cloud led him up Interstate 65 from Alabama while ravens delivered Lance crackers and Dr Pepper.

Shawn's hypersensitivity to spiritual things made my own seem normal. I'd met few people over the years whose relationships with the Holy Spirit were as weird as his.

Tony, a friend from back home, was strange in a spirit-filled sort of way. An assistant pastor at Chestertown's only Pentecostal church, Tony often shopped at the Mustard Seed bookshop. Even before he opened his mouth, I knew he was either a Baptist or a Pentecostal. His clothes gave him away. Wearing a white button-down shirt, paisley tie, and an untailored tan suit, all Tony needed was a name tag and he could have passed for a Mormon or a customer service manager at Sears.

One day he walked into the store particularly energized.

"Boy, the Holy Spirit really showed up last night at my church." Tony slapped his palms down on the counter adjacent to the cash register.

I reached to shake his hand. "Come on, Tony, doesn't the Holy Spirit always come to your church?" I showcased my trademark grin. "I thought it was a requirement."

"Well, sure, but last night was different." Tony's eyebrows started to do jumping jacks, just remembering it. "I was preaching, Matthew, and all of a sudden I felt the Holy Spirit come upon me and start moving down my spine and into my limbs. I had to stop preaching, and then God told me to waddle around on the stage like a duck!"

I couldn't speak. I just stood there and looked at him. I didn't know what the expression on my face looked like, but I wanted Tony to realize I thought he was an idiot, feelings I usually tried to hide from my friends. But not that day. I thought Tony was an idiot, and I didn't mind him knowing that.

"God told you to waddle around like a duck?"

"Yeah, you heard me right. It was as clear as anything. He said, 'Tony, waddle around on stage like a duck.'"

As he talked, I imagined what he would look like on a church stage, squatting like a duck, flapping his arms, and shimmying his backside. I'd met a good number of faith-based crazies in my day, but I'd never met anybody who waddled and quacked in the name of Jesus.

Tony continued, "So I said, 'Lord, I'm gonna obey!' And then I got down like this"—he crouched down—"and I put my arms like this"—he folded his arms and tucked his hands inside his armpits—"and I waddled and flapped like this!"

Tony reenacted the Holy Spirit's request down one of the store's aisles.

"Tony," I said, "forgive my puny Baptist faith, but why in the world would God tell you to waddle like a duck?"

"I have no idea," he said, which didn't surprise me in the least. "No idea whatsoever. But I obeyed anyway. I think sometimes God just wants to know if we're listening."

Tony told me stories like that all the time, about the Holy Spirit descending upon the stage at his church and turning it into a barnyard. But Tony believed those things served a purpose—that God was testing and preparing him for something great, something that he didn't yet understand. Chances were good, whatever God prepared for Tony, he wouldn't be the only one who didn't understand. I wondered how long it would take before I saw him and a group of his friends flapping their wings in V formation down High Street.

Shawn believed God was preparing him for something great too, so the Holy Spirit sometimes tested him, just to see if he was listening.

One of his "tests" happened as I was helping him edit an English term paper on the historical significance of Handel's *Young Messiah*. As I worked through frightfully long and dense paragraphs, I listened to 107.5, Nashville's Top-40 station. At some point Joan Osborne's song "One of Us" began playing, and I turned up the volume.

As soon as my hand left the dial, Shawn snorted. "Sorry, Matthew, but I can't listen to this song." He darted from the bed to my desk and hit the power button with the back of his hand. "And to be honest, I can't believe you're listening to it. Do you have any idea what you're putting in your head?"

Shawn's tone was heated and confrontational, a sure sign he'd spent time with God that morning. He called it his "hang time with Jesus." On certain mornings Shawn woke up early and sat in one of the campus's gazebos to read his Bible, pray, stretch, and pray some more.

I'd learned that any time Shawn and Jesus spent time together, talking and reading and stretching, Shawn was apt to make me feel guilty about something.

"Well," I said, "it's too bad you feel that way because I love that song."

That wasn't the complete truth. I wanted to love Joan's song, but at the time, I just really liked it. I was still working on being able to listen to it without feeling like I was breaking one—or *five*—of the Ten Commandments in the process. It was getting easier, but I still had a way to go.

With a year of Belmont's music business program under my belt, I had become quite comfortable listening to and even enjoying lots of popular music. Paula Abdul and Janet Jackson no longer caused my spiritual skin to crawl. I'd learned to appreciate the pitchless moans of the Red Hot Chili Peppers and Pearl Jam. I'd even mustered up enough freedom to let the melodic poetry of bands like Toad the Wet Sprocket, R.E.M., and Gin Blossoms move me in ways that Christian music often tried to do, but failed.

My roommate, Mitch, helped me get over my fear of popular music.

If campus housing hadn't put me and Mitch in the same room, I doubt we would have been friends. Or maybe it would have been easier being his friend, because I wouldn't have been forced to deal with his gastrointestinal disorder. I felt sorry for him, and in return, other people felt sorry for me. I wasn't clear on what exactly happened inside his intestines, but it made our dorm room smell like it had been deep-fried at Hardee's.

My other concern about Mitch regarded his eternal soul. He seemed to be a much bigger fan of Celine Dion and Taylor Dayne than he was of Jesus. It was a shame, really. Mitch would have made a fantastic Christian, if only Jesus had been female, sang power ballads, and released a remix album once in a while. As it turned out, though, Mitch was only as good a Christian as Madonna allowed him to be.

But he loved music. He was happiest lying on his bed, earphones on, listening to a brand-new collection of B-sides from one of his favorite divas. He boasted a collection of four hundred CDs, organized alphabetically in tall towers set along the wall space separating our twin beds, and it grew larger every Tuesday, the day record labels released new albums.

Each week, Mitch went to the library and read *Billboard, Cashbox, MusicRow,* and any other music business magazine that listed forthcoming releases, and then he hitched a ride to the closest Tower Records store, the one just five miles away from campus. Sometimes he walked there, returning home drenched in a good old Tennessee sweat. But back in the dorm room, donning his earphones, it was all worth it. In order to support his music habit, Mitch sold his blood, plasma, and any other bodily fluid that people paid money for him to produce.

Even though I thought his addiction to buying CDs was, at times, odd and unhealthy, his love for music introduced me to styles and lyrical explicitness that pushed me outside my comfort zone. Mitch taught me how to appreciate music from artists whose lifestyles I would have judged and proclaimed sinful. I'd made a lot of progress since my IBBC days, but it was still difficult to enjoy a song about God written or sung by somebody I assumed was not Christian. How could they have anything good to say about God?

Before "One of Us" released, I felt fine considering a singer's religious imagery in lyrics as blasphemous. With Joan's song, it was different; I wanted to *really* like it. Something about it allured me. Perhaps her voice, or the song's melody, or maybe the mystery of the song's message. Something kept me wanting to listen, but my ability to listen with freedom was a process. Defending Joan's song was one of the Twelve Steps.

So as I reached across my desk to turn the radio back on, I turned around and looked at Shawn. "Have you even listened to the song? I think you should at least give it a chance before you declare it blasphemous."

"I've listened enough to know that I don't want to hear it. She calls God a slob, Matthew. Is that how you think about God?"

"Wait. She doesn't *call* God a slob. She just poses the question— you know, *what if* God was a slob?"

"But that's just it; God isn't a slob. He's orderly and holy and perfect in every way. And anybody who suggests otherwise is against God and his work."

"But maybe that's why she puts it in the form of a question."

"Nonsense." Shawn scooted off the bed and stood up. "I'm really worried about you, Matthew. You're letting the world seep into your life, and you don't even know it's happening."

Shawn looked at me with the love and concern of a mother tyrannosaurus. He slapped his fist against my radio's power button and walked out of the room. The door slammed behind him.

I assumed he had passed God's test.

I sat in the school cafeteria a few days later, eating something the large ladies behind the counter described as "southern." A more accurate description might have been "unnatural," but I was hungry.

Out of the corner of my eye, I spotted Shawn approaching with a plate of pizza and salad.

"Mind if I join you?" he asked. "I have something I want to talk to you about."

I looked up and nodded.

Shawn bit into a piece of pizza as he told me about his day. He didn't mention assaulting my boom box, and I didn't bring it up.

"God has given me an idea, Matthew." Shawn grinned and stabbed his fork into a gumball-sized tomato. "I know it's God because every time I think about this, the Holy Ghost hairs on the back of my neck start to tingle."

I sighed and rolled my eyes.

"Don't get cynical on me," he said. "Just listen to my idea before you make up your mind."

I was already cynical. The last time Shawn got tickled by the Holy Spirit, the two of us were hanging out in his dorm room, debating end-times theology. More specifically, we were discussing whether or not we thought the Antichrist had already been born. Right in the middle of my argument that we weren't God and it was impossible to know for sure if the Antichrist was living or not, Shawn's face turned as white as a tube of Colgate paste.

"What's wrong?" I asked.

"Be quiet for a second," Shawn whispered.

"Why do I need to be quiet? Are you getting God bumps again?"

"Just shut up for a moment. Please?"

It was hard being quiet because I was nervous about being in the same room as whatever supernatural entity might be tickling Shawn. I bit my fingernails to pass the time.

A few moments later, Shawn looked at me. "Do you feel that?" he whispered.

"Feel what?"

"You can't *feel* that? How can you not feel that?"

"I don't know. Perhaps if I knew what I was supposed to be feeling, I could feel it."

The expression on Shawn's face turned sour. "The presence of Satan."

"*What?*"

"Satan is here."

"Where?"

"In this room."

"What? Why would Satan be in this room?"

"I'm not sure."

"Well, do you know where he is in the room?"

"No, I just feel him."

"Can you at least tell me if he's sitting on the bed? I want to move if he is."

Shawn didn't look at me. His eyes scanned the room like he could point Satan out, hiding among the plethora of Jesus knickknacks that filled his dorm room. "Somebody evil is here with us. It's either Satan or somebody closely related."

Shawn closed his eyes.

"Closely related…to Satan?" I asked.

He motioned for me to stop talking by running his fingers over his lips like a zipper.

What does he mean by "closely related"? I thought. *Are we talking about Gargamel? I'm pretty sure I can take Gargamel. Smurfs manhandled Gargamel. But if we're talking about a creature like Skeletor from He-Man, that's another story. Or was it David Copperfield?*

I closed my eyes and tried to feel what Shawn felt, but I didn't feel anything, especially not Satan. To tell the truth, I didn't know exactly what Satan felt like. I wasn't sure I had ever felt him before.

My church talked about the devil a lot, but he always seemed like Cobra from G.I. Joe—a very scary cartoon character, but still two-dimensional. Anytime Satan had shown up before, it was in inanimate objects like a Whitney Houston CD or Jordache jeans. I'd never experienced "feeling" him in a room. I got a funny feeling once after a friend forced me to listen to a Nine Inch Nails song, but I didn't think it was Satan. It was just an icky feeling, the same feeling I got whenever I saw dirty old men dressed up like Santa Claus.

"Okay, he's gone." Shawn was breathing heavily but talking at his regular volume.

"He is?"

"Yeah, I prayed him away. I told him to get out of this room in the name of Jesus."

"And he just left?"

"Yeah. Satan and his friends can't handle hearing the name of Jesus. So I kept saying it over and over again in my mind."

I wanted to roll my eyes, but I couldn't. It was hard to argue with somebody who used the ghostly presence of God as his defense, proof, and jury. Whenever Shawn's neck became a barometer for the super-natural, it was hard to take him seriously. But since I didn't know whether or not his God bumps were real, it was also difficult not to.

"Okay, so what's God telling you this time?" I asked, picking at my lunch.

"To start an accountability group! Doesn't that sound awesome? I wondered if you'd like to be in it."

"Wow, that's it? Sure. I'll try it out."

For the first time, I was actually excited about one of Shawn's Holy Spirit–inspired ideas. I'd always wanted to be in an accountability group. We didn't have groups like that back at my church in Maryland, but I'd heard a lot of Christians say good things about them. A friend once told me they were sort of like an AA meeting, except rather than helping us fight our addictions to alcohol, they encouraged our addic-tions to Jesus. "Each member in the group acts like an enabler." He assured me this was a good thing.

Because it was God's idea, Shawn appointed himself the head enabler.

"I want this to be a group where we can be real with one another," he told us at the beginning of our first meeting. "I'm hoping each of us can be honest about our struggles. And more importantly, help one another on our journeys with Christ."

On that first night, all of us were fake and lied about our struggles. Geoff struggled with whether or not he should change majors. Benjamin told us to pray for him and his girlfriend—he thought she might be the one. Andy said he needed prayer about raising money for a spring-break mission trip. Tobin struggled with soccer practice and how it got in the way of schoolwork. I confessed that the Tennessee climate was wreaking havoc on my allergies. Shawn didn't have any struggles.

It made sense that we felt leery about confessing our sins in front of other Christians, considering we had reputations to protect. I think we were all waiting for the other guy to get real.

Being accountable took a few weeks, especially because it wasn't until the fifth meeting that Shawn felt comfortable admitting his sin of hating his Church Orchestration professor.

But on the sixth week, Benjamin risked his reputation by telling the truth.

"I have a problem," he said, looking at the floor.

Everybody looked at Benjamin.

This might get interesting, I thought.

By then, I needed it to get interesting. It was nice hearing Shawn talk about how much he loved Jesus week after week, but it was also boring. Nice and boring isn't a good combination. It's like a *Family Ties* rerun—tolerable when you're home sick during the day and there's nothing else on TV except soap operas, game shows, and local news.

For me, weekly accountability had become just something to do at nine o'clock on Wednesday evenings.

"Hey, it's okay, man." Shawn patted his back. "We all have problems. That's why we have this group. As I said last week, I'm struggling to love my professor like Jesus commands. So don't feel awkward about sharing."

Benjamin looked at Shawn. "Guys, I, uh…it's hard to say."

Shawn patted his back again. "It's okay."

"I masturbate. A lot." Benjamin's eyes wandered around the room. Shawn stopped patting his back.

I was shocked. I'd never heard a Christian utter that word aloud before, at least not as a confession. Usually they described it with at least forty words, thirty-seven of them being *uh, but,* and *eh.* But Benjamin just said it, without adding any syllables or using sign language. His honesty was really quite stunning.

A funny thing happened after Benjamin's confession. We discovered that all of us except Shawn had the same problem, and most of us assumed he was lying. Benjamin's honesty changed the accountability group. My nickname for it became M.A.

Of course, Shawn felt it necessary to develop a list of code words for "masturbation," in case one of us felt uncomfortable hearing or saying the word. Eventually, we didn't even need the code words. We just held up one hand, sometimes two, signaling how many times we had stumbled that week.

We had a problem, though. None of us knew how to help each other solve our dilemma. That didn't stop us from confessing. Shawn always delivered a word from the Lord to ensure all of us felt guilty.

Our stumbling total went down on certain weeks, usually around midterms or finals, but our "problem" didn't go away.

But neither did Shawn's faith that it could.

The following semester I moved into Belmont's town houses and couldn't be in Shawn's accountability group. While we didn't hang out a lot, he and I remained friends.

One evening Shawn called; he needed to talk about something. The next day we met for coffee at Bongo Java, a hip dive with good coffee adjacent to the campus.

I arrived early, but Shawn was already sitting at a table with a cup of coffee. I said hello and then got a cup of tea.

"You don't look good, man," I said as I sat across from him.

"I'm not good. It's going to be very difficult for me to say this, but I need to tell somebody."

I almost told him that all of us figured he was lying about never masturbating, but I refrained. He had his Bible open to one of those psalms people read when they think their lives are over.

Shawn began by telling me I was his only true friend at Belmont. I found that hard to believe, since our friendship ebbed and flowed depending on whether or not he skipped his time with God, but I listened.

For twenty minutes Shawn stumbled over his words and fought back tears before getting to the point of our meeting. He was having sex with one of the interns at the music school.

"Only with our mouths," he said, placing his hand over his heart, "but it's enough to defile God's temple."

"I think God's temple will survive, Shawn. It's had to survive a lot more than this."

"But, Matthew, I gave in. Multiple times. God doesn't use people who give in. You have no idea how awful I feel. I've failed everybody. I'm a total fake."

"Shawn, you're being melodramatic. For God's sake, man, you're a human being, and human beings are sexual. And yes, in your situation, it was inappropriate and wrong, but sometimes life is messy."

"Do you think I need to stop doing the accountability group?"

"Why would you need to do that?"

"Because I'm unfit to lead."

"Shawn, you've been unfit to lead since you started that group. The only difference now is that *you* realize it. The rest of us already knew."

His face blank, Shawn looked down at the table. "I've made God look pretty stupid, haven't I?" He wiped a tear from his eye with a napkin and tried to smile. "A slob even. I've made God look like a slob."

"I guess we've all made God look like a slob at some point," I said, tracing a finger through grains of sugar on the table. "But I don't think we do that by being human. I think we do it when we pretend we're not."

Wannabe

ive months after I graduated from Belmont, I did what every other music business major did when they couldn't find a job: left Nashville and moved back home with Mom and Dad. I wasn't excited about returning to my hometown, but I told myself it wasn't my decision. It was God's.

This had to be true because when I thought about moving home, I started to feel pathetic and defeated, and my Calvinist friends assured me that this was God's way of letting me know I was in his perfect will. They said things like, "Sometimes he drags us through a little mud, and we either fight it, or we surrender and learn from it."

The only way I knew how to surrender was to let God drag me back to Chestertown and drop me off at my parents' house—*muddy*.

During college my dream of becoming the King of Kings' King of Pop fizzled out once I realized how many people came to Nashville with similar dreams. A lot of them could sing better than I could, or hung out with people who knew people who could get them noticed. Some people were called to be Christian music's version of Whitney Houston or Prince or Toad the Wet Sprocket or Celine Dion. It was rare for a person to get a call from God to make Christian music without God also giving them the name of a popular artist to copycat. Originality happened on occasion, but not often.

Timing seemed the main problem for Christians who came to Nashville to be faith-versions of pop stars. By the time God started listening to a particular artist and decided he might like to have his name associated with a particular sound, it was about four years too late. When I decided to leave Nashville in 1997, most Christians were trying to sound like Alanis Morissette, Pearl Jam, Ace of Base, or Seal.

The only people I knew who still listened to Michael Jackson performed at weddings or *were* Michael Jackson.

As I drove out of Nashville, I cried for a few miles. I decided it was time to stop feeling sorry for myself shortly after I passed the last exit for Roanoke, Virginia. Seven hours seemed like more than enough emotion over one life disaster. I told God that even though I was leaving Nashville without a record contract or a wife—the two things I most often asked him to give me—I would do my best to resist the temptation to complain.

According to the apostle Paul, half the Christian faith was pretending not to be angry and bitter about God's decisions. Hiding discontent was one thing, and I could do that; making people believe I was thrilled beyond all reason with the crappy circumstances God had given me was much more difficult. Still, the rest of the drive home I begged God to help me be content.

My parents were happy to have me home again. Even before I had unpacked, Mom and I argued about the ten o'clock curfew she thought was reasonable for a twenty-four-year-old man, and Dad put my name back in rotation for grass-cutting duty. I made it very clear that my living with them would be temporary.

"A couple of months at the most," I said. "God still has a plan for my life. He just hasn't given me the details, yet. I'll know more in sixty days." That was how long I was willing to live at home and be happy about it. Or pretend to be. I reminded God of our one-sided deal on a semiregular basis, but most of my time was spent concentrating on being happy, focusing most of my energy—physical, mental, and emotional—on remaining faithful to God. I focused any energy I had left on fighting off my father's nagging belief that God was calling me to get a job at the Visa call center in Newark, Delaware.

I managed to be happy, even excited about my future, for thirteen entire days.

On day fourteen, my sister and her boyfriend, Dave, talked me into joining a local volleyball squad of uncoordinated twenty-somethings.

Under normal circumstances I wouldn't be in a position to judge my teammates, since it was well known among my friends that most pregnant women wobbling through their third trimesters were more athletic than I was. But on this particular volleyball squad, I was one of the best players. As long as I didn't think about the fact that six out of ten team members played with the agility of coma patients, I did sometimes feel like a rock star.

After that first practice, one of my teammates and I chatted about our current lives, and he asked if I still planned to pursue a career in music. I told him I wanted to, but I didn't know what came next. Out of the corner of my eye, I saw another guy sitting next to his wife in the bleachers and listening to our conversation. As my teammate told me about his job as a plumbing technician, Mr. Eavesdropper nodded toward me, rolled his eyes, and said the word *wannabe* to his wife. She looked at me, shook her head, and said, "Such a wannabe."

Did they just call me a wannabe? But why?

Suddenly, I wasn't interested in my teammate's story about PVC piping.

Did I say something? Do they think I was bragging or exaggerating my story? Surely they aren't jealous of my volleyball skills.

I didn't know why they called me a wannabe, but I excused myself from the conversation because I felt a little sick. I wanted to march over and ask them to explain, but back then I was rarely brave enough to confront friends and family, so there was little chance of me confronting a stranger.

In the music business, being called a wannabe was a bigger deal than in ordinary situations, and I had avoided it up until that point. I worked really hard at not being a wannabe. Sure, I showed a few signs of being the Christian version of one—pride, jealousy, networking skills, maybe a touch of faith-based bipolar disorder—but that was it. It's not like I had my own Christian television show called *Joy Unspeakable and Full of Glory* on the local cable-access channel.

And I was far too young to be considered a regular wannabe. Most wannabes I knew back in Nashville were at least thirty, wore black Megadeth T-shirts, and pulled their hair back into ponytails. Often they got married just to have decent health insurance, and the majority of their kids took ADHD medication. Most of the wannabes I knew were drummers, harmonica players, or worked the soundboard.

But then it dawned on me that perhaps being single, jobless, and living with my parents made me another kind of wannabe, one I didn't recognize because it required looking in the mirror.

True Calvinists didn't look in the mirror.

"Do you think I'm a wannabe?"

My friend Cody didn't think so, but then he qualified his answer by sharing how stupid I was for moving back to Chestertown.

"Why would God tell you to move back here?" Cody took a bite of his BLT. "Makes no sense to me, especially after he went through all the trouble to get you to Nashville."

I told Cody the things I wanted to believe were true—that my time in Nashville needed to come to an end and that God had only put me back on the Eastern Shore for a short time.

"I hope you're right, man." Cody smirked.

Cody and I were new friends, but I'd known *of* him for years. The year after I graduated from high school, Cody, a pastor's kid, transferred from Queen Anne's County High School to my church's Christian school for his senior year. The story was that Cody was a rebel, and for weeks, angry church members huddled together after services and gossiped about him. He was rumored to have reached second base with his last girlfriend and did not feel guilty about it.

I think Cody's Apostolic Pentecostalism frightened them. Most Baptists thought his lack of guilt was unholy, but I thought it sounded like a pretty good reason to become Pentecostal.

Cody had grown up a lot since high school, but his maturity hadn't depleted his spiritual gift for impressing females. They fell all over him like manna fell on the children of Israel—nightly, it seemed.

Cody was a ladies' man, which I envied. I'd have loved to be a ladies' man.

Almost two years had passed since my last semiserious relationship. Being home made me want a girlfriend. There's nothing like being jobless and watching ninety-seven consecutive days of *The Price Is Right* to make you *feel* really single.

"Pentecostal churches are chock full of the most beautiful single women you will ever meet," Cody explained, selling his denomination. His theory on the Pentecostal hotness factor was related to their high success rate at converting heathens on college campuses. "Sororities, dude—that's all I'm saying. Sorority chicks who have recently found Jesus *love* me. But you have to be careful which kind of Pentecostal woman you date."

I listened with interest. "Why's that?"

"Because there are two very different Pentecostal varieties of women. The hot *nice* kind and the hot *I'd-rather-be-dating-Jesus* kind. Now you're thinking, 'Well, both types sound pretty nice to me.' But, dude, only date the hot *nice* Pentecostal woman. Promise me that."

"Okay," I said. "I promise."

"No, you have to really promise. Trust me—you do not want to date the hot *I'd-rather-be-dating-Jesus* Pentecostal woman. They are vicious creatures."

Cody's voice was strained and full of fear, like this type of Pentecostal woman had scales and a forked tongue.

"Dude, for six months I was in a relationship with this girl Sarah—a hot *I'd-rather-be-dating-Jesus* Pentecostal woman. All I can say is that she messed me up, man."

"What'd she do to you?" I asked, leaning forward.

"Expected me to be *just* like Jesus."

"Oh. Is that all?"

"*Is that all?* Dude, don't judge me until you've walked in my"—Cody stopped and looked down to see what pair of shoes he wore—"Adidas high tops."

"I'm not judging you. But don't most churches expect the same— you know, for you to be like Jesus?" I thought about my question for a moment and then added, "Well, maybe not Episcopalians. I'm not sure what they expect. But…"

"That's totally different, man. Everything I did—*everything*— Sarah would ask, 'Do you think Jesus would do that to me?' or 'Do you think Jesus would say that to me?' or 'Do you think Jesus would touch me there?' I finally had to tell her, 'I'm not Jesus!' "

I nodded. None of the women I had dated compared me to Jesus, but I did date a girl in college who broke up with me because she was convinced Jesus wanted to be her boyfriend.

Laura and I had just returned from a movie and were making out in her dorm room.

She pulled away. "I can't do this. I'm sorry. I feel like I need to be dating Jesus right now."

"Did you just say what I think you said?" I grabbed my shirt off the floor and slid it over my head. Sitting up on the edge of her bed, I asked, "So, uh, Jesus asked you out? Does he want to go steady or something?"

"Don't be mad at Jesus—it's not his fault. It just sort of happened." Laura fumbled through the bottom drawer of her nightstand and pulled out a book called *Passion and Purity* by Elisabeth Elliot. "I've been reading this book. It's so good. Did you know that, as a woman of the Lord, I am one of 'God's Little Princesses'?"

I rolled my eyes, thinking, *Well, that might be true, but three minutes ago, God's Little Princess seemed awfully excited about ripping off my shirt.*

I wasn't an idiot. I knew she didn't plan to date Jesus. She was just using God as an excuse to break up with me. But what was I supposed to say to a girl who claimed she'd been cheating on me with the Savior of the world? I couldn't get mad at her. This was Jesus she was talking about. It's not like I could ask, "Why in the world are you messing around with *that* guy?"

I told myself that Laura pretended to date Jesus because she didn't want to break my heart. Truthfully, it wasn't all that different than the two times I broke up with my girlfriend because the Holy Spirit told me to. Maybe Laura thought that using God as an excuse would make it easier for me, but really, it just made it easier for her. A month or two later Laura and Jesus broke up, and she started dating a nice-looking keyboardist from Arkansas.

I told Cody I wanted to visit his church if he thought there was a chance I might find a wife there, but I was nervous. It had been a long time since I'd attended a Pentecostal church, and I was afraid Cody's might be one that promoted the Holy Spirit with the enthusiasm that 7-Eleven advertises Big Gulps. But a change in "spiritual scenery" sounded like a good thing.

Mom and Dad had left IBBC, and the church they now attended met at the Galena Fire Department, all forty-five members. The chances of finding a wife there seemed slim.

Plus, the way Cody talked about the Pentecostal church, even with my mediocre skills with women, there was a chance I might meet a *hot* woman, preferably a low-maintenance one who didn't wear strong-scented perfumes, liked men who were poor and living with their parents, and was a *Star Wars* fan.

God can do anything, I thought.

The first chance I had to visit Cody's church wasn't on a Sunday but on a Friday evening when the church hosted a concert Cody thought I would enjoy.

"Who's performing?" I asked.

"Have you heard of BeBe and CeCe Winans?"

"I love BeBe and CeCe. I actually talked to CeCe on the phone once."

"That's mega cool, man."

"How did you guys get BeBe and CeCe to come to your church?"

"Oh, no, they won't be there, but some of their relatives will be. I hear they're very good. I think they're brothers or nephews or something of BeBe and CeCe."

"Oh." I was disappointed but agreed to check it out anyway. Cody had really sold me on the Rock of Ages Apostolic Fellowship Church, where his parents pastored.

On the night of the concert, Cody and I stood in the lobby of his church, surrounded by people donning T-shirts and carrying posters that featured the faces of BeBe and CeCe's relatives. A man wearing a blue suit and holding a walkie-talkie approached Cody as soon as we walked through the door. His name tag identified him as Geoff Forrest, Rock of Ages Security.

"Good evening, Brother Cody. I've already called tonight's seating coordinator and told her you're here." Geoff took Cody's coat and folded it over his arm. "Can I do anything else for you, sir?"

"Would you mind getting my friend and me some bottled water?" Cody asked in a tone that made him sound like one of the bratty kids from *Mr. Belvedere.*

"Of course, sir. Sparkling or still?"

"Still is fine, Geoff. Thank you." The security guard turned smartly on his heel and marched off.

"Wow," I said, my eyes wide.

Cody leaned toward me and said, "Membership at one of the largest Pentecostal churches on the Delmarva Peninsula has its privileges." He winked. "You know how we Pentecostals are, right? There are benefits when you're related to the pastor."

I didn't know much about this side of Pentecostalism, but it sounded exciting, like a Christian mafia.

A couple of minutes later, another security guard brought us bottled water and escorted us to our seats.

Since Cody was the pastor's son, our seating was reserved in the second pew. Next to me sat a middle-aged man and woman who immediately began talking to me.

"Excuse me." The man poked my knee with his finger three times. "Are you friends with Brother Cody? He's a good man, isn't he?"

I turned and looked at the man, but he put his hands over his face.

Shaking her head at him, the woman leaned over him and extended her hand. "I'm Sandra, and this is my crazy husband, Henry. You'll have to excuse his actions. He ain't right."

Henry took his face out of his hands. "Don't mind me. I'm a new Christian."

Sandra slapped Henry's thigh. "Stop acting like a freak of nature, honey. Talk to the boy like you have some sense. You're going to scare him."

"I'm sorry, mister." Henry put his palms over his face again. Then he turned toward me, looking through his fingers. "Am I scaring you?"

I smiled, and then I lied and told him I wasn't scared. What else could I say to a guy who obviously had special needs? That was the only explanation I could think of. I looked at Sandra and smiled in a way that made her think I was happy to sit next to her freak of a husband. *She must be a saint,* I thought, *or an angel, to marry a man like Henry.* I wasn't sure I had the patience to endure a relationship with somebody who behaved like him. Then again, I wasn't sure Sandra was completely "unspecial" herself.

I looked around the church auditorium for beautiful nonpsychotic Pentecostal women. I wasn't sure how to tell the difference, but I figured Cody would help.

Henry poked my knee again.

"Do you know Cody's father?" he asked. "Cody's father saved my life. Saved my *life.* I'd be dead if it weren't for him."

I nudged Cody. "Is that true? Did your father save Henry's life?"

"Henry, are you telling false stories again?" Cody's tone hung somewhere between singsong and condescending. "My father didn't save you. Jesus saved you. Isn't that right?"

I looked back and forth between Cody and Henry.

"Brother Cody's right, Henry." Sandra licked two of her fingers and then wiped some leftover toothpaste out of the corner of Henry's mouth. "Jesus saved you, baby. Cody's daddy just introduced you to Jesus."

"I guess that's right," Henry said, looking at me. "But he helped save my life. A year ago I drank a bottle or two of Robitussin a day."

"That's awful," I said, remembering how much I hated even the scent of Robitussin cough syrup. "Did you have a bad cold?"

Cody and Sandra laughed, which I thought was strange. A cold could be really annoying to a person with most of his sanity, but I assumed it might border on lethal for somebody like Henry. Their laughter made me think his condition might be worse than I thought.

"Did you have pneumonia?"

Henry shook his head. "I drank Robitussin to get high. Sometimes Triaminic, but mostly Robitussin."

"*What?* You drank Robitussin for fun? Because you *liked* it?" I'd never heard of cough syrup being used as a drug before.

"I loved the stuff," Henry said.

Sandra smiled and patted Henry's thigh. "But you love Jesus more, right, honey?" Sandra winked at Cody and returned her gaze to Henry to make sure he answered the question correctly. "You love Jesus more because he saved you and healed you, right, baby?"

Cody leaned around me so he could look Henry in the eye. "You love Jesus more than that nasty old Robitussin, ain't that right, Henry? Because he healed you."

Henry put his face in his hands again and peeped at Cody through his thumb and pointer finger.

As I watched Henry ogle Cody, I couldn't help but think that Jesus hadn't quite finished healing Henry. Maybe Henry's friends and family thought Jesus had completed his work, but I didn't think so.

When I was ten, a famous evangelist visited our church and brought his wife along for show and tell. He spent an hour telling us the story about the day his wife lost her mind. *Literally.* The forty-something mother of two woke up one day unable to speak, not knowing which state she lived in or how to walk, and she was no longer potty trained. She became like a two-year-old overnight. Doctors were stumped. Eventually it was determined that she had suffered a stroke.

The evangelist had already told us that Jesus healed his wife. They even printed the word *Miracle!* on the poster advertising his visit—the only reason he'd been invited. Stories with unresolved endings weren't popular at IBBC. We wanted the conclusions of stories to be like the ones on *Full House,* where smiles were on everybody's faces and strings played in the background.

Toward the end of his talk, the evangelist shouted at us, "But I believe, church, and my wife believes, that our Lord and Savior Jesus Christ is the Great Physician, and he can and will do miracles in your life." As proof, he invited his wife to join him on stage. While the entire congregation watched and applauded, the preacher's little wife stood and slowly walked up on stage. When she took the first step onto the platform's stairs, we gave her a standing ovation.

At that point, I was in awe of Jesus's healing ability. Then the evangelist turned to his wife and asked if she was ready. *Ready for what?* I wondered. *Did Jesus give her the ability to fly or do magic tricks?* When I was ten, that seemed like something Jesus might do—take everything away from you and then give it all back with interest.

When his wife nodded, the evangelist began reeling off questions. "What's two times two, sweetie?"

"Four," she said quickly.

We applauded.

"What's the square root of nine?"

"Three."

We applauded again. The evangelist asked his wife several more math questions, and she answered them correctly. Then he switched to geography.

"What's the capital of Nebraska?"

"Lincoln."

"What the longest river in the United States?"

"The Mississippi."

"What's the name of the mountain range that runs through Colorado, Wyoming, and Montana?"

"The Rocky Mountains."

This went on for fifteen minutes or so. Every question the evangelist asked, his wife answered with speed, sometimes before her husband had even finished the question.

On the way home my mother asked my father what he thought of the evangelist's testimony.

"It was pretty good," he said. "Seems like he's endured quite an ordeal."

Mom agreed. "It was a horrible situation, that's for sure, but I found it difficult to watch."

"How come?" Dad asked.

"I know this is going to sound bad," my mother said, "but I can't help thinking that, if Jesus had actually healed her, he would have done a better job. You know what I mean? She answered those questions like a smart poodle doing tricks."

Dad scratched his head. "I'm not sure about that, now. That seems a bit harsh."

"I said *smart* poodle. Poodles are very intelligent dogs, Virgil."

"I didn't know the answers to some of those questions."

"You would have if you'd been traveling from church to church for the last six months answering them."

"That's true, I guess."

"She seemed to just blurt out the answers, like she had them memorized. I feel bad for them, I really do. I'm just saying I would have been more impressed if she had whipped up some Rice Krispies treats or set the clock on a VCR. As it is, I thought the whole thing was patronizing."

Cody and Sandra didn't seem to be patronizing Henry's condition. He wasn't being paraded across the stage like a purple flag with the word *Yahweh* sewn into it. His story just seemed fabricated. It was obvious that following Jesus had helped him to some degree, but it wasn't a miraculous healing. Henry was in process. And there was nothing wrong with being in process. I was in process. But failing to acknowledge the loose ends of somebody's story, or pretending they didn't exist, usually caused lives to further unravel.

When Cody and Sandra finished convincing Henry that he loved Jesus more than Robitussin, he poked my knee again and offered me a toothy grin. I smiled back, but my heart felt numb.

BeBe and CeCe's relatives sang for an hour and a half, and Henry watched forty-five minutes of the show from behind his fingers.

When we left the church, Joan, Cody's mother, treated Cody, Sandra, Henry, and me to dinner at T.G.I. Friday's.

Cody always spoke very highly of his mother. She was a prophetess, he told me. He had to explain what that was, since I thought it sounded like a title that required a costume or a magic wand. Cody told me to think of his mom like a "doctor-slash-psychic" who received her "healing powers-slash-visions" from God rather than "science-slash-demons."

"She sounds interesting," I'd said, grinning. I wasn't lying. Interesting like a witch or an aborigine. I thought perhaps if I shook her hand or stood really close to her for an extended period of time, maybe she would sense something about my life or heal me of my "wannabe-ness."

As we sat down and scoured the menus, I kept looking up at Cody's mother. She didn't look like she had special powers. She looked like a mom. I kept staring at her, waiting to see if she felt anything about my future. I was too embarrassed to ask, but if she started the conversation, I planned on posing my questions: Did she think God still wanted me to pursue music? How long would it be before I met my wife? Would I stay in Chestertown forever? Was I really a wannabe?

She never said anything, so neither did I.

I ordered the Jack Daniels chicken with a side of french fries. Ten minutes after we started eating, my acid reflux started acting up, causing me to burp fire.

"Matthew." Joan looked at me with growing concern. "Do you take medication for your heartburn?"

"Yes ma'am," I said. "I take Prilosec, and it seems to work as long as I don't eat food."

Joan and I shared a laugh.

"Matthew burps all the time." Cody bit into his bacon cheeseburger. "Maybe you should pray over him, Mom."

Sandra clapped her hands. "That's a fantastic idea, Cody. Henry and I would love to see your mom pray over somebody."

"I'm willing." Joan turned to me, her eyes gleaming. "Cody knows I'm always willing to call down healing from heaven. It's a specialty."

Before I could say no thank you, Cody, Joan, Sandra, and Henry laid their hands on my back, shoulders, and head. Joan began praying.

"Jehovah God, we come to you in prayer. We come to you because you are the Great Physician. We come to you because we need your help, Father. Our dear Brother Matthew has a burping problem. The acid in his stomach doesn't know how to stay put where it belongs, God. It's venturing up his esophagus and into his throat, oh Lord…"

As she prayed, pressure formed inside my chest, a warm sensation that built in intensity.

I was going to burp. I could feel it coming.

I didn't want to burp.

Oh God, please don't let me burp. Not while Joan is asking you to heal me.

If I burped in the middle of the prayer, it might make them think I didn't have enough faith to have my ailment shooed away by God. I wanted to be healed from my acid reflux. I could definitely see the benefits. Eating would become much more enjoyable, and Prilosec was pricey.

But it was acid reflux. It wasn't cancer or heart disease or even high cholesterol.

Acid reflux is sort of like gingivitis. You don't want it, but it's probably not going to kill you. I wouldn't even have known what to call my condition if I hadn't seen a commercial about it.

Faith in situations like this felt forced. I was used to faith happening accidentally, usually when I wasn't thinking about it. But in that moment, as four well-intentioned crazy people asked God to heal me of my stomach woes in the middle of T.G.I. Friday's—which seemed a little like asking God to take away sex addiction while standing in a strip club—I tried to have faith.

And by "having faith," I mean I concentrated really hard on my stomach. With my eyes shut, I kept saying over and over again in my head, *Heal my stomach, God, heal my stomach.*

After saying that about fifty times, I actually started wanting God to heal my stomach. Liquid fire in the back of your throat was unpleasant, but mostly I wanted to be healed so I wouldn't have to pretend I was healed until dinner was over, and then for the entire ride home with Cody.

Just when I thought it couldn't get worse, Joan began speaking in tongues, which excited Cody, Henry, and Sandra. They whispered phrases like "Praise you, God" and "We give you glory, God" and "Yes, Jesus" as their hands squeezed my shoulders, neck, and back.

It felt like getting a back rub from an octopus.

The only time I'd heard Cody sound so spiritual was once when he talked about having sex. I'd never heard him be so passionate about God.

It was during the part in Joan's prayer when she asked God to reach his hand down my throat and soothe the insides of my stomach that I remembered we were at T.G.I. Friday's.

What must these people be thinking?

Even with my eyes closed, I was certain people glared at us. I was sure they were looking at us, wondering what I had done to warrant such an intervention.

"And God, in Jesus's name, we ask you to cast out this acid reflux. We

say, 'No, Devil, not today!' You can't have Brother Matthew's stomach from today on! From this moment on! Because in the name of Jesus, be gone!'

After Joan said amen, we continued eating. But instead of chatting, the four of them stared at me, waiting to see if I burped.

I excused myself so I could go to the bathroom and belch.

"Are you okay, man?" asked Cody after I returned from the rest room a second time.

"Yeah, I'm fine."

He smiled. "Awesome. God is good."

"You can say that again, son," said Joan.

I smiled and sat down.

"God is *very* good." Henry poked my knee three times. "Look what he did to me!"

I looked at Henry. When he grinned, his face glowed with a light I wasn't sure I understood. I just knew he seemed to experience a joy I didn't know. For the last few months, all I seemed capable of doing was sitting around and making lists of things God had failed me on.

Henry put his hands over his face and peered at me through his fingers. "Matthew," he said, "both of us have been healed!"

A gurgle of acid bubbled in my stomach as Henry's words made the truth clear: I was a wannabe. And the only one sitting at the table.

Chance

In 1998 I became the manager of Jammin' Java, a coffeehouse on Maryland's Eastern Shore with the motto "Music, Coffee, and Community." My mother said, "Wow, you might actually use that music business degree we paid for after all." It seemed like a decent possibility, since my job included booking talent for the Jammin' Java stage.

Having a salaried job was a nice change. God's little tractor-pull-through-the-mud had become exhausting and humiliating, though occasionally entertaining.

Four months after moving home from Nashville, I started working *emotionally* hard labor as a substitute teacher for fifth through eighth graders. On a couple of occasions I feared for my life, but mostly, after learning the stories of the kids I baby-sat, I feared for theirs.

When the school year ended, my father landed me an eight-week temporary job, one that required traveling to every dairy farm in Kent County and trudging ankle deep in cow poop so I could collect manure samples. Then I took the poo back to the office and tested it for soil-damaging chemicals. The job was crap, but learning about cows and the sometimes-unhealthy poo they produced was far more enjoyable and interesting than I would have imagined.

After that, I spent eight months earning $6.75 per hour stuffing envelopes next to people with no high school education and poor hygiene in the darkly lit warehouse of a local fulfillment center.

A second Jammin' Java location opened in the suburbs of DC in 1999, and I moved from the Eastern Shore to northern Virginia in order to take the manager position.

Late on a Monday afternoon I'd just finished booking the last spot for Open Mic night when a woman with big, frizzy hair and sunglasses walked up to the sign-up table.

"Are you the manager?" she asked.

"Yes," I said, "how can I help you?"

"I'm Tina." She sighed loud enough for the whole coffeehouse to hear her. "I'm trying to figure out if I'm in the right place." She pulled a scrap of paper out of her back pocket and uncrinkled it. "This is the Christian coffeehouse, right? The one I hear mentioned on the Christian radio station?" She inched her sunglasses down low enough that I could see the purple eye shadow plastered above her eyes. "I don't see it posted anywhere. I thought it would be posted."

"What's not posted?"

"That this is a Christian coffeehouse."

I forced a smile. People made similar remarks all the time. "Well, actually we prefer not to call it a *Christian* coffeehouse."

Tina pulled the sunglasses off her face. "What? Why wouldn't you jump at the chance to call it Christian? Are you ashamed of your faith?"

As many times as I'd been asked that question, I still didn't know how to answer it without making somebody angry or eliciting more questions. Our reasons for not advertising Jammin' Java as a Christian coffeehouse came down to semantics, really. Using the word *Chris-*

tian as an adjective went against the owner's theology. And since my boss was a multimillionaire, his theology tended to be more biblically accurate than other people's theologies.

"Just because I'm a Christian," he'd told us at least a hundred times during staff meetings, "doesn't mean everything I do or make or support *is* Christian. To me, that's nonsense. Does a farmer who happens to be a Christian grow *Christian* tomatoes? Of course not. That's ridiculous. In relationship to the tomatoes, his Christianity is little more than a technicality."

Some people countered by suggesting God blessed a Christian farmer's tomatoes with more flavor or better color than the tomatoes grown by non-Christians, but my boss thought that was hogwash.

His thinking might not seem like a big deal today, but back in 1999, raging against the use of "Christian" as a modifier was considered "new" and "edgy," like praise and worship leaders who highlighted the tips of their hair. A lot of evangelicals didn't know what to think of a Christian who refused to describe things like bookstores, movies, T-shirts, and culture as "Christian." While I didn't understand why some thought it was controversial, it often made describing the concept of Jammin' Java difficult, especially to somebody who didn't care about the proper use of adjectives or, for that matter, theology.

After I finished explaining our reasoning, Tina asked another question.

"So you're saying it *is* a Christian coffeehouse, but you just don't call it a *Christian* coffeehouse, is that what I'm hearing?"

"No, actually it's a coffeehouse owned and operated by people who love Jesus."

"And how is that different from calling it a Christian coffeehouse?"

"The difference is just sentence structure."

"But basically you are a Christian coffeehouse, right?"

I groaned silently. "Yes, we're basically a Christian coffeehouse—minus the fluorescent lighting and church basement location."

"Okay," she said. "So this is a safe place for Christians to hang out?"

I smiled again. "We don't stone them here, if that's what you mean."

Tina laughed so hard that she told me her stomach hurt. "You're funny." Regaining her composure, she asked, "Where do I sign up for Open Mic night?"

I explained that all the spots for that evening were booked. "But you can come back next week, Tina! We'd love to have you."

Tina looked like she no longer thought I was funny.

"What?" She threw her hands up in the air. "I drove all the way here! More than thirty minutes with traffic. Now I have a horrible headache. You have to let me play."

I looked down at the list and pretended to consider letting her play. "Aw, Tina, I wish I could, but the spots are all full," I said, apologizing again, as if it was my fault twelve other people had beat her to the sign-up table.

"You could let me play," she said. "Is there somebody else I can talk to?"

"No, unfortunately. I'm the manager."

"Unbelievable."

She stomped out the front door.

I understood Tina's passion. I was the lead singer of a five-member band named Our Mutual Friend. I stole the name from a novel by Charles Dickens. I liked to think of the "mutual friend" as Jesus, which seemed a lot less cheesy to me in 1999 than it did in 2001. But people liked our music and thought we were destined for Christian music stardom—a good sign considering we'd only played one gig.

As it turned out, only two of us were really into the idea of making it big. Slowly, over the course of three and a half weeks, the band broke up. Chris, the acoustic guitar player, had a wife who didn't like being alone on weeknights. Payton, the bass player, quit because he entered Christian rehab to recover from his issues with anger and pornography. And Simon, the most talented drummer/percussionist I have ever met, quit because he started hitting on the girlfriend of Wade, our electric guitar player. I told Wade that I didn't want to be a Christian rock duo—too many bad memories. But for two months, Our Mutual Friend rocked.

Tina returned a few minutes later carrying a purse, guitar, and a Diet Coke. She dropped her belongings on a table adjacent to mine and then stood a few feet away from me and looked around the coffeehouse like she was a lost buffalo, accidentally wandering into civilization while looking for Nebraska. A few moments later, Tina placed her hands on the sign-up table and leaned in close enough that I could smell dinner on her breath.

"I see now why you don't advertise this as a 'Christian' coffeehouse."

I braced myself, thinking I was about to know what the money-changers experienced when Jesus caught them selling stuff in the Lord's temple. I didn't think Tina would try to toss me out the front door, but I wouldn't have been surprised if she called me a "viper" or "whoremonger." But instead of flipping my table over and throwing my clipboard across the room, Tina tapped her fingernails on the tabletop.

"I'm thinking," she said, passive-aggressively flapping her glittery eyelids at me.

I pushed my chair back. "What are you thinking about?"

"Oh, just how I'm going to get you to let me play my songs tonight." She stopped tapping and straightened, crossing her arms. Tears formed in the corners of her eyes. "Why won't you let me play? Seriously, why? I wore this flashy new shirt just for tonight. I made it myself."

I had to admit her shirt was nice, a navy blue cotton T-shirt. I assumed the "flash" she referenced was the word *Jesus* she'd BeDazzled across her bosoms. Whether or not God's son liked his name written in cheap gemstones and stretched between two mammary glands, I didn't know. But her message was bold and her bosoms quite bountiful.

"Ma'am, I'd love to let you sing."

"Oh, please. You're just being mean." Thrusting her hand into her large purse, Tina felt around like she was performing an endoscopy. "Okay, so you're not in that corner. Maybe you're over in this one." As she pushed her hand to the opposite side of her bag, she glared at me.

Her stare didn't faze me.

Jammin Java's Open Mic night notoriously attracted interesting, untalented characters. Many coffeehouses and bars advertised Open Mic nights, but I'm pretty sure that ours was the only local stage where, once in a while, Open Mic night seemed more like a casting call for Christian crazies than a display of artistic endeavor.

We started Open Mic night to offer local musicians a fifteen-minute chance to shine. A few did shine, but usually, audience members not related to the musician headed for the door to make phone calls, smoke, or offer their ears a bit of mercy. Most of the people interested in getting behind our microphone were forty-something musicians Jesus had saved from drug addiction, alcoholism, or playing guitar in a Led Zeppelin tribute band. I was thrilled Jesus had shown the old rockers how to live without drugs, alcohol, and bar gigs, but it would have been easier on our ears had he also given them talent.

Tina moved away from me and dumped her purse's contents onto another café table. "There you are!" She snatched a photograph out of the pile. "I knew you were in there somewhere."

With the photograph in her hand, she walked back to my table. "I want to show you something, Mr. Turner." Tina plopped the picture down on the table in front of me and pointed at the face of a pretty, thin thirtyish-year-old woman with auburn hair and smooth skin.

"That's *me*," she said confidently.

"Okay," I said, "but what does that have to do with you playing tonight?"

"I'm getting there. You can see a big difference, right? That's because this was taken ten years ago. Before my divorce. Before I caught my husband in bed with another woman. And before I gained one hundred and twenty-*two* pounds."

I looked up at her.

"But, honey, I'm doing all right. It's just me, my twelve-year-old son, and Jesus! And we make it. Yes, we do."

Tina got down on her knees in front of the table, eye to eye with me, and pleaded. "Mr. Turner, my music is all my son and I have. When I woke up this morning, God told me to go to Jammin' Java. He said, 'They're Christians there, Tina, and today is the first step toward making that music career you've always dreamed about into a reality!' And God does not lie. You know that, and I know that, so please, don't make God into a liar."

"Tina, listen—" I told her that I was not, under any circumstances, putting her name on the playlist. In fact, after those dramatics, I wouldn't have put her name on that list if somebody had canceled.

"But if you would like to come back next week," I said, "call ahead, and I'll make sure your name gets written down."

"Fine." She folded her arms. "It's your loss. I know lots of people in this town, and I plan to make some phone calls! And you're missing out, because I can really sing! I sound like a mix of Janis Joplin and Mahalia Jackson."

"Well, come back next week, Mahalia, and we'll let you play."

Tina packed up her belongings and stormed out.

Tina didn't show up for Open Mic night the following week. I wasn't too sorry about that, but I did feel bad about our heated exchange.

A few months later, I received a message on the Jammin' Java's answering machine. As soon as I heard it, I knew it was Tina. Her tone was professional and as sweet as pecan pie.

"Hello, Mr. Turner. This is Tina Larson. I hope your staff and you are having a very blessed day today. You and I had the pleasure of meeting a few months ago. I was the passionate little filly who wanted to sing on Open Mic night. I'm very sorry for portraying myself like I did. I hope you'll forgive me. I'm calling to see if I can meet with you tomorrow to discuss the possibility of being the opening act for Ashley Cleveland on the twenty-first of this month. I've already discussed this with Ashley's people, and they love the idea. They said as long as it's okay with you, I would be welcome to play a fifteen-minute warmup set. I hope to hear from you soon. Bye!"

I called Ashley's people immediately. Pam is a good friend of mine, and if she approved Tina to open for Ashley, I would honor her request in a heartbeat.

"You were on my list to call today, Matthew," Pam said after a quick exchange of hellos. "Who, pray tell, is Tina Larson?"

"According to the voice-mail message I received this morning, she's Ashley's opening act. Which was, as she tells it, approved by you."

"Good Lord, are you kidding?"

"Afraid not." I filled Pam in on my first encounter with Tina. "To say the least, she's a bit of a loose cannon."

"Sounds like it. Do you have any idea if she can sing?"

"Nope. But I think she and I are meeting today."

"Well, you know Ashley—she doesn't care if Tina opens for her or not, but it's your call. Not mine."

That afternoon Tina and I met, and the first thing I noticed was the sparkling diamond stud she had stuck through a hole in her nose. She caught me staring at it.

"Do you love it?" Tina rubbed a finger over it. "Pretty cool, huh? I got it for my forty-fifth birthday. It makes me look younger, doesn't it?"

I smiled, asked her to excuse me for a moment, and walked slowly back to my office. Rummaging through the top drawer of my desk, I found my bottle of Excedrin Migraine caplets. I popped four in my mouth and washed them down with water. I took a deep breath, walked back out to the table, and sat down.

"So what did you think about my exciting news?" Tina's eyebrows rose to her hairline. "Can you believe Ashley's people invited me to open for her? I about peed my pants when I got the e-mail!"

Everything inside me wanted to scream at her. I wanted to call her a liar, revel in her misfortune of my friendship with Ashley's people. I wanted to tell her I knew the truth about her so-called invitation to be the opening act. But something stopped me. Not exactly mercy. Something a little more human and less refined.

"Me too, Tina. I'm looking forward to hearing you sing. You can do three songs."

Tina smiled. "You want to hear a secret?"

"Okay, sure.

"Ten days after my Ashley gig, I'm going in for the Carnie Wilson surgery." Tina threw her hands up and shook her palms. "You know, the surgery that makes people skinny. I can't wait."

"Oh Tina, I'm speechless, and that doesn't happen too often. But I really don't know what to say."

"Say 'Praise Jesus!' Matthew, because I'm going to look fabulous again when it's all done."

Tina smiled.

I didn't want to praise Jesus about it. Gastric bypass surgery was still new then, and I'd heard a lot of scary things about it. Lots of overweight people praised it, but it was a risky method to look, as Tina said, fabulous.

"I'll be fine," she said. "Seriously, I will be okay. God told me I'd be okay. My surgeon is one of the best in the country. And I've got a music career to go after."

On the evening of the Ashley Cleveland concert, Tina wore a new homemade shirt and the tightest stonewashed jeans I had ever seen on a woman with cankles. BeDazzled across her boobs were the words *God's fava*.

"Do you love my shirt or what?" she asked me in the greenroom right before she went on.

"It's a nice shirt, Tina."

"Did you see how many people came from my church? Ten! Ten people. And my mom's here. She hasn't heard me sing in years."

"Are you ready?" I asked. "You're on in two minutes."

"Yes, I'm ready."

I turned to walk onto the stage to introduce her.

"Matthew." Tina put her hands on the back of my shoulders. "Thank you so much for this opportunity. You'll never know what it means to me. I feel like tonight is the beginning of something beautiful for me."

And for a moment, Tina's smile glittered more brightly than the words on her T-shirt.

I knew what she felt. Letting her play three songs on a stage with lights in front of people, I was giving her a chance to prove herself. That's like winning the lottery for an artist.

Once, in college, I was given a similar opportunity. A friend of a friend hosted a songwriter's night at a coffeehouse in Nashville similar to Jammin' Java. Based only on the fact that we had mutual friends, the man offered me ten minutes to perform two of my own songs.

In the days leading up to that evening, I was a nervous wreck. Because people of influence and fame often attended, I viewed those ten minutes as the beginning of something. I imagined that, after hearing my songs and seeing the audience's reaction, somebody from a record label or a management office would approach me at the end of the evening and tell me I had talent. I pictured that person inviting me to sign a contract that stated my talent belonged to them, that they would take my talent, make as much money as they could with it, and offer me a small percentage of the profits. Which sounded heavenly.

On the day the contract was signed, cameras would flash all around me as I put my signature on the official documents. Upon signing my life away, the person who discovered me and I would hug and then eat cake. My fantasy looked a lot like a wedding.

Two friends came to my show, Veronica and Kevyn with a *y*. That's how he introduced himself to everybody—"Hi, I'm Kevyn with a *y*." On his birth certificate his name was spelled with an *i*, like all the normal Kevins I knew.

"The *y* makes me more interesting, Matthew," he told me. "It's artsy."

I couldn't argue with him. At the time, I was on a campaign to be called "Thew," as in "matTHEW." Every Matthew at Belmont went by "Matt," so in an effort to be different and interesting, and also to help in classroom situations with four or five Matts in attendance, I tried to make my family and friends call me "Thew."

It never caught on.

"I thought you were pretty good," Veronica said when I finished singing and returned to our table. "Your voice isn't bad at all."

Veronica was a music performance major at Belmont University, so I knew how to translate her compliment. She meant that, while my voice was tolerable, I had no chance whatsoever of getting a record deal. Kevyn with a *y* was more blunt.

"Your songs are depressing, man," he said. "Seriously, I wanted to ask one of the baristas for the Yellow Pages so I could write down the names of a few therapists."

I raked my pitch-black dyed hair with my fingers. "Whatever, man. You're such a typical Christian—you only want your Jesus to come in bubblegum flavor."

"Don't get defensive just because your songs make me want to take Prozac."

After the other songwriters finished performing, I waited around to see if anybody wanted to "talk." Nothing happened. I was disappointed that nobody liked my songs enough to have a conversation with me. It felt like I was back in high school, the last person chosen to be on a soccer team. Except it hurt more, since I couldn't play soccer but felt totally convinced I was a decent singer-songwriter.

But I had the chance to perform, and I was grateful.

I was nervous about Tina's chance, since I'd never heard her sing. It was a stupid gamble on my part, one I hadn't made before.

When she walked on stage, Tina plugged in her guitar, sat on the stool, and strummed her guitar. After four strums, she sang her first line.

It was painful. Most of the performance followed in the same way. Once in a while her voice accidentally fell on key, but it tripped again soon after. When somebody can't carry a tune, and you're forced to endure three pitchy songs, time always seems to stop and rub it in your face. It's actually possible to lose track of what day it is.

About two and a half minutes into Tina's fifteen minutes of melodic torture, I cried uncle. I couldn't look at her, afraid I might not be able to hold back my *you're an ungodly bad singer* expression. I kept my gaze fixed on her mother, who was smiling. And apparently deaf. But I could tell she was proud of Tina and perhaps thinking she was watching a new beginning happen for her daughter. I think all of us hoped for the same up until the moment we heard her singing voice.

After that, we just hoped to survive long enough to hear Ashley.

Tina ran up to me after her performance. "Well," she said, "what did you think? Did you love me or what?"

Oh God, I thought, *quick, what would Jesus do?*

Would he be blunt? Would he explain that, for some reason beyond his understanding, his father decided against giving her the talent she so desperately wanted to possess? Would he heal her vocal cords?

Since I didn't know how Jesus would handle a situations like this, I did what I believed was the most Christlike thing to do. I lied.

"You were unbelievable," I said, wearing my Christiany smile. "I was blown away."

I should have stopped there. I didn't need to say anything further. Jesus would have stopped lying at that point, but not me. I kept going.

"You have a real gift, Tina," I told her. "You might seriously have a career in this. It won't be easy, but it's possible."

"So I might be able to come back after my surgery and have my own show at Jammin' Java?"

"Of course. I'm sure I'll be able to make something happen."

While Tina chatted with other people, her mom walked up and put her arms around me. Her hug made me feel awkward. People began to stare. It was like being the only human in a room full of hungry grizzly bears. Rather than offering a full-frontal hug in return, I hugged her sideways and patted her back.

"Thank you for giving Tina this opportunity," she said, finally letting go.

"Oh, it's my pleasure, ma'am."

"I don't think you understand." She blinked, trying to rid her eyes of tears. "I don't know if you realize this or not, but Tina's had a very difficult few years."

I nodded.

"She's been depressed and angry off and on for years. I've worried about her for a long time. Frankly, I'm still worried about her. I don't know if she told you about the surgery she's having, but I'm worried about that. I don't want her to have it. But you can't tell that girl anything. She's stubborn."

She sighed. "Oh, I don't mean to waste your time going on and on about this. I just wanted to say thank you for tonight. My little girl is happier than I've seen her in years, and it's been a tall glass of mercy for me."

I put my arms around her, this time embracing her fully and without fear. I stopped feeling guilty about lying to Tina. I didn't feel good about lying, and I would no doubt receive phone calls and comments from audience members offended by Tina's lack of talent, but I didn't care. I made a pact with myself to remember the words of Tina's mom if somebody called to complain.

On her way out the door, Tina thanked me again and told me that the next time I saw her she would be a whole lot skinnier.

"Well, make sure your mom calls and lets us know how it goes," I said.

Two weeks went by and I forgot about Tina and her surgery. I only remembered when one of the staff members told me that Tina's mom was on the phone.

"Hello, Mrs. Larson," I said when I picked up the phone. "How's Tina doing?"

There was silence on the other end, the worst kind of silence. I heard sniffling, and then a deep sigh.

"I lost my little girl today, Matthew. She's gone." Then the sound of a mother's anguish. "I lost my little girl."

Four hours after the doctor completed what he called a successful surgery, Tina's heart gave up. Doctors and nurses tried to save her, but her heart remained stubborn, and soon she was gone.

There's nothing like somebody's untimely death to make your life feel small and meaningless. My three encounters with Tina were uncomfortable. On each occasion, I had to work to relate to her or tolerate her. The weeks following Tina's passing, I struggled to get the thought of her out of my mind.

I thought about her odd behavior, the nose ring, her BeDazzled T-shirts, her unpolished singing voice. I hardly knew the woman, and yet for some reason, I couldn't get her out of my head.

Sometimes I pictured her sitting in heaven, playing her guitar and singing off-key for God. Oddly, the thought gave me a little hope, wondering if perhaps Tina had been right.

Maybe her gig at Jammin' Java really was the beginning of something beautiful.

Chasing Amy

Look what I just got."

Michael stood at the door to my office and waved a CD at me. I didn't know what he was talking about, but the smirk pasted across his face told me that whatever was on the CD, I wanted to hear it.

"What did you get?" I asked.

"Get your butt to the conference room," he replied. "We're gonna have ourselves a listening party!"

I loved a good listening party. A gathering of two or more people hearing new music from a Christian artist, listening parties were one of my favorite perks of working for *CCM*, a magazine covering Christian music.

The acronym *CCM* stood for "contemporary Christian music," which doesn't mean much anymore, but at one time CCM was a genre that included any kind of "churchy" music that wasn't a hymn or written prior to 1964, the year Bill Gaither wrote the song "He Touched Me."

Despite a title that sounded like something siblings might whine from the backseat on a long road trip, "He Touched Me" became a huge hit in churches across America and catapulted Bill Gaither's singing and songwriting career to Christian empire status, which happens to include lots of treasures here on earth. I've heard some people describe Bill as the Elvis of Christian music—not in sound but in influence—and others refer to him as the Tony Bennett God loves. Either way, Bill's song connected, and not only did millions of Christians want God to touch them like he touched Bill, that song's success led a multitude of people to write torch songs to Jesus.

I was *CCM*'s editor, a position I wasn't qualified to hold. I had no proper training in editorial or writing, and the only experience I had that even remotely related to my job description was eight months as a content editor for the music and entertainment page at Crosswalk.com, a Christian Web site. As it turned out, my unqualified status worked in my favor, because ignorance lowers people's expectations.

When the publisher of *CCM,* a fifty-something man named Gerald who only listened to southern gospel music, offered me the job, I was shocked. But I accepted the offer, and for the first time since graduating from Belmont, I lived in Nashville again.

Most of us at *CCM* thought we were cool, which, of course, meant we thought others considered us cool too. I'm sure most of us thought that a good percentage of Christians in Orlando, Dallas, and South Bend, Indiana, envied us because of our jobs. We were a powerful and influential group of people among Christian music's elite.

That wasn't saying much unless you live in Franklin, Tennessee, a small town thirty minutes outside Nashville, where the majority of Christian music was recorded, packaged, and endorsed by Jesus, but it meant something to us. We were in Franklin all the time. Meetings, lunches, and coffee with tobyMac and tobyMac's publicist.

As I walked into the conference room, Michael put the CD in the stereo.

"Okay, whose music is this?" I sat in one of the swivel chairs surrounding the table.

"I'm not telling," he sang. "But trust me, you want to hear it."

He was likely right. We didn't have listening parties for every artist. Impromptu celebrations were reserved for the artists we liked, seven or eight "faithful" talents we deemed *really* good and not simply *Christian* good.

Michael pushed Play. As he sat down, he folded his hands and looked up. "God, please let this be good. She *needs* this to be good."

I looked at him. "Wait a minute. Is this…"

Michael grinned. "Maybe."

The first song began, electric guitar riff with some percussion.

"How in the world did you get this?" I asked.

"I've got my ways." Michael leaned back in his chair and put both hands on top of his perfectly round, bald head. "And I can't tell you or somebody might die."

"Right. Because this isn't supposed to be available to us for another month."

"I know." Michael couldn't stop smiling.

An unmistakable voice began singing over the music, a once smooth alto that life and maturity had made noticeably raspier.

Michael began yelling at the stereo. "Come on, Amy! The songs need to get better than this if you're gonna compete with the youngsters!"

"Let's pick up the tempo a bit, Amy," I added.

Michael and I looked at each other, knowing what the other was thinking.

"I'm getting worried," said Michael.

"Me too, but let's not jump to conclusions. It's only the first song."

"Yeah, but it's not a good song, Matthew! It's not *dreadful,* but *'not dreadful'* is not good enough. Amy needs a hit song! And preferably one that isn't about Christmas." Pointing at the stereo, he added, "What radio station is going to play this?"

I shrugged. "Probably none."

Leaning over, Michael pushed the skip button to track two and then stood and paced around the conference room. At the intro to the second song, he threw up his hands. "Oh, come on, Amy! What *is* this?"

I sighed. "Oh no. Do you hear the effects on those background vocals?"

"You mean the ones that were cool in 1998? Yes."

Michael and I were friends because of Amy Grant. She didn't introduce us, but our strong love for her became a foundation on which to build our friendship.

One of the best aspects of knowing each other was being able to talk about our frustration when one of Amy's songs didn't showcase the talent we knew she had. We could freely ask questions and discuss our doubts about certain songs or lyrics. Michael and I trusted each other, so we didn't fear saying anything that would cause the other to give up on Amy. We knew that no matter what either of us said, we'd both still buy every album Amy released and listen to them over and over again until we learned to love every single one of her songs.

We also both believed in refraining from talking negatively about Amy around people who were unsure of their relationship with her or were still on the fence. Both of us dreaded even the thought of saying something that might cause a longtime Amy fan to not buy her latest CD.

My friend Shellie had been obsessed with Amy for years, but she was beginning to worry me. She'd become one of those people who called herself an Amy fan but showed no enthusiasm about her relationship with Amy. The last time we chatted, she confessed that she hadn't bought Amy's latest greatest hits album.

"I looked at it in the store," she said, and in an attempt to backpedal out of the hole she'd dug, she said, "I just decided that I didn't need to buy it because I already had all of the songs."

I hardly knew what to say, but I did my best to lay the guilt on thick. "You have *all* of the songs?"

"Of course I have all of the songs."

"Do you have them on compact disc? You realize the mixes are new, right? And all of the songs have been remastered."

"I have all of the songs on CD, Matthew," she said.

"Even 'Old Man's Rubble'? I know very well you don't own 'Old Man's Rubble' on compact disc."

At one time Shellie's devotion to Amy put mine to shame. The stories she told were hilarious. In college she told me that at her first Amy concert in 1985, she stood in Amy's autograph line for more than two hours in a gymnast's leotard. When she finally reached the signing table, she asked if Amy was interested in seeing some amazing gymnastic skills. Of course Amy said yes, so fourteen-year-old Shellie threw off her coat and put her hands in the air. She dipped into a handstand, sprang forward and flipped two times, cartwheeled once to her feet, and concluded her routine by dropping into the splits. As soon as she finished her floor exercise, Amy applauded.

Before hanging up, I asked Shellie if she remembered the time she and I, along with a few friends, drove around looking for Amy and Gary's ranch until three o'clock in the morning.

"Sure, I remember that. Why?"

"Do you remember what we stole from outside her gate?"

"A tulip. A *yellow* tulip."

"You don't still have it, do you?"

"*No,* I don't still have the tulip."

The second song on Amy's new album began to grow on me and Michael. Musically it wasn't all that original, but the lyrics drew us in.

"She gets so confessional at times," Michael said. "On a couple of her songs I've thought, *Oh Amy, why do you always have to be so honest?* Don't get me wrong. I love that about her. But most of the time people rip her apart for it."

"This song seems especially honest." I turned the volume up. "Don't you think this song has to be about the divorce? It is, right?"

He listened for a moment, and then his eyes widened. "You don't think this song is in reference to the interview you did with her last year, do you?"

I leaned closer to the stereo's speakers, as if that helped me concentrate on what Amy was singing.

The interview Michael referred to happened when Amy released her first album of hymns. I volunteered to write the story. A few days before the interview, I received an e-mail from Gerald, my publisher, asking me to come to his office at my earliest convenience.

Just reading the e-mail caused my heart to beat like a conga drum. Gerald frightened me. At least half of what came out of his mouth was meant to break somebody down.

I deleted the e-mail and told myself to think of Gerald's office like Daniel thought of the lions' den. *God will shut the lion's mouth,* I thought as I poked my head into his office.

"Gerald, can you talk now?"

Without looking at me, he said, "Yeah, come on in."

He threw an old copy of *CCM* on his desk in front of me. It was the issue with Amy on the cover, and the interview inside focused on her divorce from Gary Chapman.

"Have you read this interview?" Gerald asked.

"Yeah, I read it."

"Pretty pathetic, isn't it?" He thumbed through the pages of the interview, waiting for me to agree. When I didn't say anything, he looked up. "Well?"

"How is that interview pathetic? I loved that story."

"She doesn't apologize, Matthew. For getting a divorce." Gerald shifted in his chair. "Not one time. It's as if she's not sorry for disobeying God's command to stay married. She needs to apologize."

He closed the magazine.

"Who does she need to apologize to, Gerald?"

"Her fans. Us at *CCM*. And everybody she failed."

Our chat went on like this for fifteen minutes. Eventually, Gerald got to his point.

"On Wednesday when you do the interview, get her to apologize. *Ask* her to apologize if you need to."

"Are you kidding me? You're asking me walk into Amy's house and get her to apologize for something that happened more than three years ago? She's remarried, Gerald."

Gerald threw his hands in the air. "I want her to apologize."

"Gerald, this isn't Watergate. We cover Christian music. Can't we do a fun story and let the stupid divorce topic remain in the past?"

"God has rules." He spun his chair toward the laptop sitting on a table next to his desk. "Either get Amy to apologize or we won't run the story. Period. Get out of here."

I walked out.

Two days later, as I pulled into Vince and Amy's U-shaped driveway, my stomach ached at what Gerald wanted me to do. I shifted the car into park and began to panic. *I'm getting ready to interrogate Amy Grant. I love Amy Grant. I want her to love me.*

My relationship with Amy was already strained, and the two of us hadn't even met. I blamed my mother for that.

The first time I heard Amy was when my sister Kelley dated a heathen from her Christian college who let her borrow his mixed cassette tapes of Christian rock songs. I was eleven. Kelley only let me listen to two of the songs on the tape, but I memorized them both.

One of the songs was called "Heartbeat," sung by a Canadian artist named Connie Scott. Connie was the Olivia Newton-John of Christian music, and "Heartbeat" was God's "Let's Get Physical." Connie's song didn't promote casual sex, though; she just borrowed all of Olivia's keyboard sounds to create her song.

The other song was Amy's version of "Sing Your Praise to the Lord," written by Rich Mullins and with a Bach-inspired introduction. I listened to that introduction over and over again one afternoon and felt like I was in heaven until my mother stormed into my bedroom and stole Amy out of my possession.

When it came to music, Mom was as likable as the Grim Reaper. I was convinced she hated Amy, but perhaps she was just afraid of Amy. Her fear-driven meanspiritedness wasn't her fault. People at church told Mom that Amy was actually Madonna dressed in Christian*ish* clothing, which meant she bought her clothes at the Deb Shops but still fraternized with the devil.

Mom and I argued a lot about Amy. On my sixteenth birthday, I convinced her to let me buy Amy's 1983 *A Christmas Album* only because she figured Amy would have to be pretty sick to sexualize Jesus's birthday.

In the spring of 1991, eight months before I turned eighteen, *Heart in Motion* released. The buzz about this record was huge, as it was Amy's first real push to create an album that anybody—Christian or otherwise—might enjoy.

I worked at the Mustard Seed bookshop at the time. In the corner of the store's music section stood a five-foot "Amy" floor display, advertising the new release. There was no way I would be able to wait until I could vote and fight in wars to listen to Amy's new record.

However, my mother thought otherwise.

"I didn't let you listen to her Christian rock stuff," she said. "What makes you think I'd even consider letting you buy her *secular* pop record?"

It didn't matter that in the last song, "Hope Set High," Amy sang about her faith in God and even used the word *Jesus* several times.

Mom was stubborn. "You are not bringing that filth into my house."

So I bought *Heart in Motion* with my own money and hid it underneath the front seat of my car. A month later, Mom found it and stormed into my bedroom like an avenging angel, armed with a pitchfork and a cassette tape.

"What is this?" she screamed. "What is this?"

My pale face turned from pasty to transparent. "It's the Amy—"

"I know what it is! I specifically told you not to bring this junk into this house."

I didn't say this, but *technically,* Mom brought it into the house. She yelled at me for fifteen minutes. It saddened her that I disobeyed her wishes, that I thought because I was old enough to drive, I could get around the rules she deemed appropriate for me. She went on a long tirade about how much I had changed in the last few months. And then she burst into tears and exited my bedroom dramatically.

I tossed *Heart in Motion* in the garbage.

But I loved that record, and my life didn't feel complete without "Baby Baby," so I bought it again, a month after the argument with my mother.

I felt guilty about my purchase, and the stress of keeping something from my mother got to me. On a day when I felt particularly close to God, I threw away my new copy of *Heart in Motion.* A few hours later I regretted that decision, so I went outside and rummaged through the garbage, found the tape, and put it back under the front seat of my car. Two days later, the anxiety of my sin was killing me. That time I broke the Amy cassette in two, stuffed it into a bag, and then tossed it in the trash can. But a few weeks later, I missed it.

So I bought it again.

That time, when I started feeling like I was hiding a dead body underneath the front seat of my car, I tossed the tape out the window. Then I felt guilty for littering.

This cycle repeated four times, which meant I purchased *Heart in Motion* a total of five times.

An hour before my interview with Amy, my mother called to ask if I was excited. Mom's loosened up a lot since the early nineties. During the summer of 1996, she even went with Elisabeth and me to an Amy Grant concert.

While talking, I reminded her of the *Heart in Motion* debacle.

She groaned. "I was so miserable back then," she said. "Please don't tell Amy that story."

I told her I planned to tell Amy every single detail.

"Just make sure you tell her I've changed since then, all right? Please. Would you at least do that?"

"I'll pray about it," I said, half kidding.

I rang Amy's doorbell and stood on her front steps, trying to look casual and carefree. When that didn't work, I checked to make sure I wasn't sweating through my shirt and doused my mouth with mint-flavored spray. As I heard footsteps approach, I offered up a desperate prayer:

God, help me to not make a fool out of myself.

Help Amy get ready to say she's sorry to people she hasn't sinned against.

Please make her like me.

God's response was simple. "Uh, Matthew, Amy likes everybody."

When Amy opened the door, I hesitated. I needed a moment to realize the experience was real and not one of the dreams I'd had so many times of meeting Amy, only to be arrested a few minutes later because I wore only my underwear. In my subconscious, Amy met me in my underwear hundreds of times.

After greeting each other and shaking hands, Amy led me from the front door into the kitchen. "I made corn chowder, and we're having bread bowls—a nice southern meal."

Amy's warmth and hospitality put me at ease. Her kind, down-to-earth spirit made interviewing her easy. It was more like having a chat with an old friend. Of course, the whole time I thought about my publisher and his mandate. I kept hearing his gruff voice in my ear. "If she doesn't make a public apology, then she's not going in the magazine."

After discussing everything from family and music to Nashville and the theology behind the celebration of Lent, I forged into more troubling waters.

"Amy," I said, "can I be honest?"

"Sure. Of course."

"The next couple of questions are not mine. And if I had any choice in the matter, they wouldn't be asked."

Amy didn't take her eyes off me. She nodded politely and then laughed knowingly. "I wonder where this is going."

I rolled my eyes.

Then I got blunt, though I stuttered through my question. "My publisher thinks you got off easy the last two times *CCM* interviewed you. He seems to think that, because you got divorced—an act that is biblically frowned upon—you failed your fans. So I'm supposed to ask you this: Are you willing to apologize to your fans and to *CCM* magazine for divorcing Gary?"

The question was met with a long period of silence. Awkward silence. Painful silence. I felt like I was slowly killing her. When she began to answer the question, she stopped and started several times.

"Do I feel sorry because my life hasn't turned out like I thought it would," she said, "and because of that, I have fans that feel disappointed or betrayed? Sure. I never make a decision without considering how it will affect the people in my life. Sometimes I do that to a fault."

I watched her think about my question and then consider her life—how it was before her divorce and after—and it was obvious she wasn't beyond feeling sorrowful about her divorce. But even to someone who just met her, she clearly had found redemption for the decision, and she held onto it. My question couldn't steal that away from her.

"The hardest part for me, Matthew, was forgiving myself. But once you do, you can't keep going back. You accept the grace and live."

That evening Amy invited me to visit with her at the recording studio. When I arrived, she stood inside a small soundproof room with a headset on, rerecording vocals for her hymn project. A few feet away from the couch I sat on, Vince adjusted dials on the console. Sitting next to Vince was Brown Bannister, Amy's longtime friend and record producer.

As Vince fiddled with controls, Brown chatted with me about Amy.

"It's a thrill for me to hear Amy sing these old hymns, Matthew. The other night Amy laid down vocals on 'He Leadeth Me.' What an experience. I cried. So pure, so full of life. I sat right here and had an altar call."

Amy started singing.

"I have to get right with God nearly every time I hear that girl sing," Brown said.

Everybody in the room stopped what they were doing and just listened. Brown closed his eyes. I laid back against the couch and soaked up the experience of hearing her sing "Softly and Tenderly."

Come home, come home; Ye who are weary, come home.

It took me two weeks to write the story. When I finished, I printed it out and slid it under my publisher's door.

A few minutes later, Gerald called me into his office. I considered putting on a bulletproof jacket, or at the very least, wearing a wire so somebody who liked me could eavesdrop on our conversation. It was very possible I might need saving. In my opinion, Gerald was the worst kind of bully—a gruff, condescending, loud, biblical literalist.

I sat in one of the two chairs in front of his desk. Gerald's face remained glued to his laptop as if he didn't even know I'd entered the room. No hello. No nod. Nothing. When he finished typing, he swung his chair in my direction.

I felt like I was middle school again, my literature teacher critiquing my book report on Dickens's *Great Expectations*. "You think you can relate to Pip's story, do you?" she said. "Humor us, Matthew; how do you think your life resembles Pip's sad existence? Go on; tell us."

Gerald picked up my story and leaned back in his chair. "I suppose you think this is a good story, don't you?"

I looked directly into his passive-aggressive eyes. "I love the story," I said. "I think it reveals where Amy is. It's an accurate portrayal of what she thinks and believes at this point in her life."

Gerald leaned forward and rested his elbows on his desk. "I don't care where Amy is in life. And I don't think our readers care either."

"I disagree. I think they do care. If they don't, then why in the world do we print a magazine that assumes they do?"

"You're missing the point. This story doesn't reveal the Amy I want our readers to know. This story practically condones divorce."

"It hardly condones divorce."

His face turned purple, making him look like a teakettle about to announce its boiling point.

"Don't contradict me, Matthew. I know what I read. This article right here condones divorce."

"With all due respect, Gerald, I don't know what you're talking about."

"There's no apology! That's what I'm talking about. I'm not printing this trash." Gerald folded the pages of the story in half and threw them at me. Papers fell around my feet.

As I picked up the papers, tears formed in my eyes. When I had gathered the story, I calmly placed it on the corner of Gerald's desk. He looked at it and slid it onto the floor again.

"Get that story out of my face."

I gathered the loose sheets of paper and walked out of Gerald's office.

Amy's face still graced the cover of *CCM* that month, but the printed story only loosely resembled the one I wrote. Gerald forced my editorial director to rewrite the story. The new story featured Amy miraculously apologizing. Her quotes were fabricated and molded into something that didn't represent her story or my story, but rather a story that reflected the moral absolutes Gerald believed *CCM* hadn't upheld until he was in charge.

According to Gerald, the truth about Amy just wasn't Christian enough to be put in the pages of his magazine. I'm not sure anybody's truth was worthy of Gerald's *CCM*.

The last few chords of the final song on Amy's new record came to a close.

"So," I said, "what do you think?"

Michael looked at me and shook his head. "She's not afraid to tell the truth. Were you listening to the song about losing her innocence? So amazing."

Over the years Michael's and my affection for Amy had grown, and as thirtyish adults, our feelings for her far surpassed the label of mere "fan." Being called Amy's "fan" insulted us. "Fan" implied celebrity. Amy was much more than a celebrity to Michael and me. We considered her to be more like a sister. She was our storyteller, one who often shared our narrative. And sometimes she felt like a modern-day John the Baptist.

Of course, calling Amy our "voice in the wilderness" didn't come without sacrifices: the name-calling, the laughter, the severe teasing, questions about our masculinity, and sometimes doubts about whether or not our ears worked. But those were sacrifices any fan of Christian music had to make, regardless of who they listened to.

Christian music didn't make you cool; it made you *feel* cool. Like beer and jean jackets. And much like drinking beer and wearing jean jackets, the cool feeling Christian music brought to one's life usually faded.

The story of Michael's early years is nearly identical to mine. Different parents, different churches, different states, but our experiences were the same. Both of us were raised Independent Fundamental Baptists. When we met people who hadn't heard of our form of Baptist, we told them it was Christian for "scary beyond all reason."

By the time we turned twelve, Michael and I were convinced we knew everything there was to know about God. If that information wasn't already stored in our brains somewhere, our parents had flashcards to help us memorize it. People who told us that God was more or less than what we'd been taught were liars sent by Satan to deceive us. Our teenage years brought questions, college brought doubt, and we spent the better part of our twenties in therapy, trying to reconcile our understandings of God, sex, relationships, and what we believed to be true.

But there was one consistent thread of grace in our lives, a trail we could follow all the way back to when our memories began: music. Music reminded us that we could trust God even when "his people" failed us.

And at some point, our paths crossed with Amy's music, which gave both of us hope that God wasn't nearly as hateful as we'd been taught.

Michael pushed the eject button on the stereo's CD player. "I'll listen to it a couple more times and probably love it."

"Same here." I stood up and stretched.

After all, listening to Amy felt like coming home.

Real Fake

Allison's voice sounded shaky when I answered my cell phone. I wasn't surprised by her tone. Everything about my friend Allison was shaky at one time or another—*shaky* was in her DNA. Out of breath, she somehow still managed to shriek into the phone like a bikini-clad cheerleader from an eighties horror flick, and I held my phone at arm's length in hopes of understanding her muffled screech.

"I can't understand a thing you're saying, Allison," I said bluntly. "Please lower your voice and slow down."

"Sorry," she said. "I'm just so upset."

"What's wrong?"

"It's James, Matthew."

My blood pressure dropped to a normal rate as I realized chances were good that no immediate danger existed. Allison reacted hysterically about anything regarding James.

The two of them had history, having "courted" for a year. This basically meant that James and Allison acted like they were dating; they just weren't committed. At some point Allison mustered up the courage to ask James about his intentions. He told her he didn't know what she was talking about, that as far as he was concerned, the two of them were just friends.

Since then, Allison had turned into James's stalker, and James had turned into a jerk. The whole thing was very complicated, but at least James and Allison were no longer the only two people in our circle of friends who didn't realize it was complicated. That fact didn't make it less complicated, but it did up the entertainment value.

"What's up with James now, Allison?"

"He dropped out of the band and is moving to California."

"Who told you this?" I asked, knowing the chances of her and James having chatted were slim.

"Wait, I haven't told you the worst part. He claims he's no longer a Christian. He's calling himself a recovering Christian. That's apparently why he's moving to California—it's part of his recovery."

"There's a silver lining in all of this, you know."

"I don't want to hear about the silver lining, Matthew. I'm worried about James."

"No, that's just it, Allison; you're not worried about James. You're worried about you. And while I'm sad about James moving, I think it will be fantastic for you."

Four days passed before I could talk to James. We met at the Green House. At the time, the Green House was one of the popular places in Nashville where people who worked in the Christian music industry went to smoke clove cigarettes and get drunk. James suggested we meet there, which I thought odd, considering he was no longer a Christian and no longer had to keep his encounters with alcohol under wraps.

"I might no longer be a Christian," James told me, "but for another month I'm under contract with a Christian band, and I feel like I should follow the rules so I don't hurt the band's future."

That made perfect sense to me. I knew lots of people contractually obligated to act like Christians. Most of them considered themselves Christian, but their type of Christianity didn't warrant airtime on religious radio stations or get them invited to play in front of church youth groups. Hence, why the Christian music industry invented contractual Christianity—it kept band members honest. Or at least sober.

"What's going on inside that head of yours, man?" I grabbed my bottle of Amstel Light and knocked its neck against the neck of his Corona. "I'm not here to judge or try to talk you out of leaving Nashville. I just want to know why."

James didn't say anything at first. He just stared at his beer and watched its sweat drip down to the cardboard coaster. "It's complicated."

"You gotta do better than that," I said, taking a drink. "I mean, you're leaving your music career to move to California."

"Are you kidding? You call what I have a music career?" James chuckled. "What I do ain't a career. It isn't even a ministry. You have no idea how tired I am of the frickin' politics of the Christian music industry, Matthew."

I just listened and watched the bubbles in my drink dance to the surface.

"Don't pretend not to know what I'm talking about, Matthew. You've been around this industry long enough—you used to be the editor of *CCM* magazine, for God's sake." He raised his bottle casually and added, "But soon I'll be done with it all. No more dealing with gatekeepers. Thank you, Jeeeesus."

Then he took a long, slow drink.

I knew who James meant by "the gatekeepers." At least I talked about them like I knew them. Everybody who worked in Christian music talked about "the gatekeepers," like a committee of grizzled old white men who sat in a boardroom somewhere in Texas, bent on making life a living hell for any Christian who made art for a living. Nobody ever said their names aloud. I'm not sure we knew any of their names. The industry's gatekeepers were like a secret society—wizards of Oz—powerful and influential people who controlled what was said and who was allowed to say it.

"Oh, come on, James, we don't even know who these 'gatekeepers' are. Or if they really exist. Why are you letting them chase you away from Nashville and your faith?"

I tried really hard to not come across as judgmental, but I also felt a certain responsibility to ask James the difficult questions. Most of his other friends hung around him because he was a musician and they were wannabe musicians. Nashville is full of people who befriend the famous or the semifamous in hopes of finding celebrity themselves. In turn, a lot of artists and musicians seemed almost to feed off their relationships with groups of talented and likable yes-men.

I recognized this in other people because I was guilty of the same thing on so many occasions. My friendships with talented, rich, and influential people didn't always begin with bad intentions, but often I easily became lost in the hope that a friendship would help me to succeed. In James's case, his friends were like leeches who didn't dare disagree with him, lest they lose their place in sucking order.

But his talent and popularity didn't do anything for me. I'd already been through that phase.

"Oh, they exist, Matthew," said James. "I've met one of them."

"You met a gatekeeper?"

"Yep, about eight months ago."

I had so many questions: Was he old and white like we assumed? Was he aggressive? Did he have fangs?

"I met him in Dallas on a radio tour. He's tall and old and looks like a cowboy."

"Wow, I'm so jealous. How do you know he's one of the gate-keepers?"

James rolled his eyes. "Because we were sent down there by our record label to kiss his butt. They told us if he decided to play our single, it would become a hit."

"Did he play it?"

"Nope. He said our song wasn't Jesusy enough. I think he uses an equation to figure that out."

"Oh. Sorry."

James shrugged his shoulders. "I don't care, man. I'm done. Moving on to new and better things. I don't want to deal with this industry anymore."

"I get that," I said. "But why have you suddenly become agnostic?"

"Well, I don't know if I'm agnostic, really." James hesitated. "I'm not even sure what being agnostic means. I just think I'm trying to figure out what I believe. I know I don't fit into Nashville's version of Christianity."

"And you think you'll fit into L.A.'s version?"

James nodded. "From what I hear, L.A. doesn't have a version. They hate Christians out there, so I'll fit in quite nicely." He smirked as he took another drink. "Quite honestly, Matthew, I'm just sick of being the guitar player who travels around in a beat-up minivan, putting on pep rallies for Jesus. It's just so plastic and fake."

"Do you think you're going to find 'real' in L.A.? Even the boobs are fake there."

James thought for a moment and then quipped, "But that's the sort of 'fake' I don't mind." He hollered at the bartender and ordered a second drink. "That might make me a hypocrite, but at least now I'm being honest about my flaws. That's more than I can say for most of the Christian musicians in this town."

James wasn't being judgmental, just honest. Honesty can sometimes sound judgmental to those who don't fully understand the topic of conversation. But James knew firsthand what it meant to be a Christian rocker, a talented believer who received more attention and praise for his virginity than for his guitar skills.

When he first decided he wanted to play in a Christian rock band, James had no idea that, as long as he remained unmarried, he would be expected to discuss his lack of sexual history with large numbers of strangers. Other than Tim, the band's drummer, James was the only nonmarried person in the band.

"Last night I received a standing ovation for being a virgin," James once shared with me after a gig at a Christian music festival in Texas. "Those Texans sure like their virgins. Fifteen thousand people applauded my chastity for seven minutes."

"Really?" I squinted and tried to remember the conversations about sex James and I had had over the years. "But wait. You're not really a virgin, are you?"

"Technically I am."

"Technically you're a virgin? You're a virgin because of a technicality?" I knew what he meant. Technically, I was a virgin too. But I was too interested in hearing James's explanation to let him out of this conversation so easily.

"Yes, I'm technically a virgin," he said.

"How can somebody *technically* be a virgin?"

"Easy. I've never—you know—done the deed. Signed the papers. Parked in the garage. Put my offering in the offering plate. Are you with me?"

James's voice cracked, which meant he was uncomfortable.

"Yes, but…"

"No buts. That's all that matters. Because the pig never got in the blanket, I'm 'technically' a virgin."

"But did you explain this technicality to those fifteen thousand people? I mean, just because it's a technicality doesn't mean it's not important."

"No, I didn't offer any explanation. Our manager says youth pastors aren't interested in details."

"Interesting," I said. "It doesn't make any sense, but it's certainly interesting."

"What are you getting at?"

"I think the crowd deserves to know the whole story, that's all." I looked at him with forced judgment in my eyes, trying not to laugh. "You know what I mean? I'm just not sure that the real question here is whether or not the pig got in the blanket. I think your applauders would be interested to know if the pig was next to the blanket. And ultimately, did the pig get warm?"

"I hate you," James said, realizing by the grin spreading across my face that I was giving him a hard time. "You have no idea how much I hate talking about my 'virginity.' I feel so stupid and cheesy. I didn't become a musician so I could give speeches about abstinence."

"You guys should let Tim give the talk!" I said, believing I'd come up with a perfect solution. "He's the drummer, single, and from what I could tell, very comfortable in front of people."

The look on James's face said he was holding back pertinent information.

"What? Has Tim's car been parked in a garage?" I asked. "Technically speaking, of course."

"No. His car hasn't even seen a driveway."

"Well, then he seems perfect for leading the crusade against parking in garages."

James rolled his eyes. "You would think so, wouldn't you? But Tim weighs three hundred pounds."

"Why does that matter? Fat people have sex too."

James laughed. "That's not what I'm getting at."

"Then why did you bring up Tim's weight?"

"Promise me you will never repeat this to anybody."

"Oh, I won't tell a soul," I said. "I promise this will just be between you and me."

He sighed. "A few months ago the band actually talked to our manager about having Tim do some of the virginity presentations. But he said no because he was concerned that youth groups wouldn't be as impressed with Tim's virginity as they would be mine."

My mouth hung open as James explained why his manager believed Tim's virginity wasn't as marketable as his. It was simple vanity. "He's afraid teenagers might look at Tim and think that his untouched status has less to do with his belief in Jesus and more to do with the fact that nobody wants to see him naked. He says that, since I'm skinny and have muscle tone, my 'virginity' appears more faith-induced and, therefore, sellable."

"Your virginity is up for sale?"

"You know what I mean," said James. "Our manager says lots of Christian bands make calculated decisions like this. It's just the nature of the business. It's why you rarely see a fat girl up on stage promoting chaste behavior; it's not as impressive."

"So because you look like somebody who could score if he wanted to, your quest to remain pure is seen as heroic and faith filled? Is that what you're saying?"

"Yeah, I guess," he said. "When you put it that way, it doesn't sound as nice as the way our manager puts it."

The Christian music industry had long been obsessed with virginity, so I wasn't surprised to hear that managers created business strategies on how a talent could best capitalize on their passion for purity. Purity was a hot commodity. Christian artists and bands who boasted about their virginities on stage at large youth events often sold more CDs, T-shirts, and stickers than those who didn't.

In 1995 I volunteered to do stage security at a Christian music festival in one of Nashville's ritzier suburbs. It was my job to walk to and from the stage with the artists and protect them from the occasional mob of Jesus-loving thirteen-year-olds—a pretty simple task.

One of the performers assigned to my protective custody was a young high-schooler named Rebecca St. James. A new singer from Australia, hardly anybody even blinked an eye at Rebecca when I escorted her from the greenroom to the stage area. She was only scheduled to perform three songs.

After her second song, she sat on the edge of the stage and told two thousand people—mostly teenagers—that she was a virgin. It seemed a little out of place. None of the other artists had discussed their sexual inactivity, and I didn't hear anybody from the audience ask. But Rebecca must have known that people were curious about her, sitting on their blankets, thinking, *I wonder if this girl is a virgin*. I assumed this was true, because as soon as Rebecca confirmed her virginity, the crowd erupted into thunderous applause. All across the festival's lawn, people rose to their feet in celebration of Rebecca's garage having never seen a car. A few people backstage clapped for Rebecca too. Eventually I stood and applauded. For three minutes, we gave Rebecca a standing ovation.

The excitement surrounding Rebecca's virginity was far more than I had ever felt for my own. I rarely thought about God being pleased by my virginity. I'm not sure he was pleased. I'm not sure he really thought about it. I certainly don't believe he desired me to make a living from it. I think James had come to the same conclusion, but he was also tired of being fake about his passion for remaining chaste until marriage.

Looking back, I'm pretty sure he was just tired of being fake.

When I left the bar, I concluded that James didn't know what he wanted. He just knew he no longer wanted to live in Nashville and didn't want to associate himself with Christianity, at least the Nashville kind. He told me he needed to get away from his current life so he could figure out what he believed to be true about God.

"I might become a Buddhist," James told me, "or maybe I can turn into a Jew or join one of those Hollywood religions that get advertised in the personal ads out there. Who knows? I just know I don't want to do this anymore."

For a moment, I considered backing out of my former promise not to try to talk him out of leaving. But I took a couple of deep breaths and told myself not to panic, that James leaving Nashville was not as big of a deal as it felt like it was. I knew lots of former Christian musicians like James, tired of trying to make a living within the hoopla of Christianity.

Six weeks later I helped James pack his car for his move. I was sad about his departure, mostly because I feared what L.A. might do to him. Several months after that, I was in California for a speaking engagement, so I met James for sushi.

We hadn't chatted since he left Nashville. When I called, I wasn't sure he would want to hang out. Right after Christmas, he'd sent out a mass e-mail that rather glowingly expressed his New Year's resolution to give up trying to befriend Christians. I hadn't taken offense at his e-mail, but I did wonder whether or not I was one of the Christians he'd sworn off.

I left a message on his voice mail. A few hours later, James called and told me that he'd love to meet.

"Even after your New Year's resolution?" I asked.

"Of course," he replied. "Your Christianity is pretty harmless, Matthew." I could hear his grin over the phone.

I didn't know how to take that. I was partly relieved, since it meant he still wanted to be my friend, but I was also mildly put off by his comment. According to a lot of churches, Christians aren't supposed to be harmless. A lot of pastors think we're supposed to be more like soldiers—brave and courageous and able to leap to big conclusions in a single sentence. But by that time, I was beginning to rethink what it meant to be Christian. My faith was becoming less like a get-out-of-hell-free card and leaning more toward a way to live. Because of Jesus,

I wanted to love people, which meant I didn't want to engage in relationships with an agenda.

A week later I sat with James at a sushi bar in Southern California. In the e-mail he sent out, James had described himself as a recovering Christian. I'd met a number of people going through a similar healing process. A couple of things seemed to happen when an individual attempted to recover from his dependence on Christianity: (1) he became a know-it-all about everything, and (2) he became a fan of Tori Amos. James had both symptoms, which indicated his recovery was going quite well.

"Matthew." James used chopsticks to pick up a piece of smoked salmon on rice. "I've met too many Christians who make Jesus seem like a caricature of Hitler rather than a loving God. If God really equaled love, then I might still be Christian."

An atomic bomb went off in my chest. "You think Christians make Jesus seem like Hitler? That's a bit extreme."

"I don't think so." James shook his chopsticks at me and chewed his food. "I'm convinced that if Jesus is anything close to how the Bible describes him, then he and I would probably get along. We might actually love each other. But his people? His people are fake. Nobody can tolerate his people, Matthew. You don't know how much better I feel now that I'm out of it."

I poked my fork in a California roll.

"You know, man," said James, "I sometimes wonder if Jesus might consider himself a recovering Christian like me."

I thought maybe James had a point. Maybe Jesus was tired of being a Christian. Perhaps our ways of celebrating him were too limiting. Maybe I was a part of the problem and not the solution. Maybe Jesus was chilling with James at one of those expensive rehabilitation resorts where famous people go to overcome addictions. Maybe they were poolside, telling each other war stories.

And listening to Tori Amos.

Allelvia

I'm awake on Easter morning long before my alarm goes off. Jessica and my nine-month-old son, Elias, are in Wisconsin, spending the holiday weekend with my in-laws. I like time alone, but any more than two days without my family and my brain becomes restless. Jessica and Elias have been gone since Thursday, and I'm starting to talk to myself.

Gawking at my reflection in the mirror, I wonder aloud if it's sacrilegious to attend church wearing all black on Easter Sunday. I like black, but I don't usually wear *all* black. I fear that somebody might think I'm Sin and throw a bucket of lamb's blood on me. It's unlikely, I know, but even at the most "relevant" churches, Easter Sunday can become a Christian's full moon.

I decide I'm overthinking it, that my black garb doesn't make me look like Iniquity, but rather like somebody who waits tables at O'Charley's. But between my own words of affirmation, I hear my mother's voice in my head: "Is that what you're wearing? On Easter Sunday? It's not a funeral."

And that's all my imagination needs, to create a make-believe argument with my mother.

"I like what I have on," I think back at her.

Mom shrugs, but only with her eyebrows. "Fine."

"What?" I think more loudly than before. "Am I twelve? You can't tell me what to wear to church."

"I'm not saying a word. Not a word. If you want to go to church looking like somebody who thinks Jesus is still dead, that's fine with me."

"Fine. I will."

A few minutes later, at eight thirty, my alarm clock goes off and the first thing I hear is a church choir singing "Christ the Lord Is Risen Today." Even though churches only sing this hymn on Easter Sunday because it takes until Christmas to get the refrain out of your head, I love hearing it. There's something irreplaceable about two-hundred-year-old hymns on Easter. Later this afternoon the melody will make me want to beat my head against the wall, but for now, it makes me think about Mammom.

After my grandfather passed away in 1984, she lived with my family. Nearly every morning Mammom walked into the kitchen singing the words of an old hymn. It didn't feel like morning unless I could smell Dad's strong pot of Maxwell House brewing and hear Mammom quietly singing about Jesus at the breakfast table. She died in 1995, but her singing voice remains safe in my memory. Low and quiet and aged ninety years, I hear Mammom's voice sing "Christ the Lord Is Risen Today."

Listening to that beautiful sound play over and over again in my mind makes me forget about the argument I imagined with my mother. However, it also shames me into rummaging through my closet and smelling every pair of khakis I own in hopes of finding a clean pair to change into. Eventually, I stand in front of the mirror again—singing along with Mammom—wearing a black short-sleeved pullover with tan pants.

I don't look as springlike as some of the men in my church, who will no doubt come ready to celebrate Jesus's resurrection dressed in Easter-egg colors. But the tan pants do make me look brighter, and I think my mother would approve. I don't need her to, but I don't avoid her approval like I did for a while. Not in person, anyway.

A few minutes before ten o'clock, I leave for church.

I'm still singing.

I arrive thirty-five minutes early for the second service at Cross Point Community Church. The first thing I notice upon walking into the auditorium is how empty it is, which surprises me since it's Easter, and written in last week's bulletin was an announcement to arrive early because seating was limited. I'd never have seen the "warning," but my wife's Type A personality comes fully equipped with a love for reading bulletins, newsletters, and pamphlets of information. She doesn't feel like she's been to church unless she's read the bulletin cover to cover.

I find a pew, sit down, and watch well-dressed families and individuals enter God's house. So many colors, bright and happy, and accented with frills. It's like watching a bag of Brach's jellybeans parade down the aisle. And so far, I'm the only person wearing licorice.

A few minutes later, a man wearing a strawberry-shaded polo and dark jeans with fancy stitching on the front pockets stands at the end of my pew. "Excuse me, is this seat taken?"

He might be thirty, but I doubt it. His demeanor is kind, but the white shoes he's wearing are atrocious.

"The seat is all yours, man," I say. We smile and nod at each other like I'm sure Jesus would do.

"Thanks." He sits down and smiles so big that half his face disappears behind his teeth. Holding the bulletin in one hand, he puts his Bible in the hymnal shelf on the back of the pew in front of us. "I've never been to this church before, and for some reason I'm a little nervous."

He turns toward me. "It's been a while but I told myself that I couldn't skip church on Easter. Because it's *Easter.* I've never missed church on Easter. Never, except for last year." He exhales loudly and adds, "It's been a long year."

"I understand," I say. "I've had a long year too."

He is nervous. I watch out of the corner of my eye as he folds his arms and then unfolds them, puts one leg on top of the other and then puts both feet on the floor. I know all too well what it feels like to visit a new church for the first time. I always feel self-conscience and unprotected, like the first time I had to get cleaned up after gym class in a community shower. I was in seventh grade and I looked like I was in third.

"Yeah, being the 'first-time visitor' sucks, man," I say. "By the way, I'm Matthew." I reach out my hand to shake his.

"Yes, it does." He glances up for a moment and then looks at me again. "Wait a second, I've seen you before. I have totally seen you somewhere before."

I roll my eyes and prepare to be mistaken for the guy in the Verizon Wireless commercials. It's not that I look like him so much, but I'm thin, have a receding hairline, and wear black-rimmed glasses, so once in a while a random person comes up to me and says, "You're the 'Can You Hear Me Now?' dude, aren't you?" It usually happens at airports when I'm on my cell phone, but it's never happened at church.

I grin and shake my head. "I'm not the Verizon guy, man."

"What? The Verizon guy? What are you talking about?"

"You think I'm the 'Can You Hear Me Now?' guy, right?"

He looks confused. "Why would I think that? You look nothing like that guy."

I feel stupid for mentioning it. "Okay, so where have you seen me before?"

"Oh, I know where I saw you: At Vanderbilt the other night. You know, author night with Augusten Burroughs! *Love* him, by the way. But you were there—with your wife, right? She's short, pretty—*really* cute haircut. That was you, wasn't it? You sat in the second row! I know it was you."

Suddenly I feel socially violated. He knows what my wife looks like, and that seems weird. I begin to wonder if this guy—*who still hasn't given me his name*—is a stalker. I'm not sure why somebody would ever stalk me. Once, a forty-five-year-old inmate in an Alabama prison wrote me four letters in a span of six weeks to tell me he loved my book *The Christian Culture Survival Guide.* My wife called him "my husband's stalker" when she talked to other people about the situation, but I never felt scared or "followed." Then again, I hadn't sat next to him at church before either.

In an effort to appear calm and unalarmed, I bite my fingernails as I ponder if I should excuse myself to the "bathroom."

"What's your name?" I ask.

"Oh, I'm sorry," he says. "My name is Kyle."

"So, Kyle, you *saw me* at the Augusten Burroughs event? There were a lot of people in that theater."

"I know," he says excitedly, oblivious to the fear in my eyes. "But I remember you because you hugged my favorite Christian music artist of all time, Margaret Becker. That was you, right? As soon as she arrived, you two hugged, chatted, and hugged again. I was so jealous. I'm the biggest Margaret Becker fan in the entire world."

I felt better—and a bit saddened that the possibility of having my very own stalker vanished so quickly. I wasn't worried about Margaret's safety. The New York–born Christian singer-songwriter has been making faith-based rock and pop music for more than two decades, so she was used to having stalkers. Margaret and I aren't best friends, but we've known each other for more than ten years. When we met, I was booking talent at Jammin' Java, and I booked Margaret and her band three or four times while at that job.

"Margaret and I know each other," I tell him. "I've been a fan of her music since the early 1990s. In my opinion, she's one of the best songwriters in music—of any genre."

"I agree," says Kyle. "She's frickin' *brilliant*! I love her. You don't understand. I have been through so many moments of complete hell in the last year. I relied on so many of her songs to get me through some of the lows." He stops talking and thinks, but only for a moment. "What are the chances that I would sit by you on Easter Sunday? It's so cool." His voice becomes louder *"And it's all because of Maggie!"*

Kyle and I share Margaret stories for another five minutes or so. I'm always inspired when I hear about an artist's influence on a person's story. I think it's because I understand that connection.

"My gosh," says Kyle, "do you know how long it's been since I've had a conversation about Christian music? Or music in general, for that matter." Kyle folds his hands and stares toward the corner of the church auditorium. "There was a time when I wanted to do music."

"What kind of music?" I ask.

"*Christian* music," he says. "Well, the stuff I love to sing is praise and worship music."

I laugh. "I'm pretty sure that's still considered Christian music. Wait, I take that back. I have definitely been in situations where worship music unto God was about as Christian as Pop-Tarts."

I look around and realize the auditorium is full. A timer appears on one of the big screens: it seems in ten minutes, Easter Sunday will have liftoff. I direct Kyle's attention toward the timer.

"A countdown, eh?" says Kyle, laughing. "If the stage set is any indication, it looks like it might be like Broadway."

"It will try, Kyle," I say. "The church had a dress rehearsal for Easter this past Tuesday."

"My church back home had dress rehearsals for every Sunday."

"It'll be big. Pete, the pastor here, is a friend, and he's already warned me that I'm going to *hate* the light show."

"That's hilarious that the pastor actually warned you."

"I know." My eyes catch a glimpse of the timer. I lean in so I can whisper, "Kyle, I'm pretty sure that in seven minutes and twenty-two seconds, Jesus is going to bust out of a tomb somewhere in this room and declare victory over sin."

Kyle smiles as he watches one of the guitar players kneel on stage and tune his guitar.

"This reminds me so much of my church at home." Kyle looks at me. "I used to be one of the worship leaders at a pretty large church in Tampa, and sometimes I miss it. I loved connecting with people. And you know, music does that. I think there's something very unique about how you connect with people through worshiping God, especially for the person leading. It's powerful."

"And you don't do music now?"

"Just at home." Kyle breathes deep and lets it out slowly. "But even at home, I don't sing too often. I stopped doing music in public, like eighteen months ago."

"How come?" The two words come out of my mouth despite knowing that my question is nosy, but I feel like I'm supposed to ask. Then again, maybe I'm just being nosy.

A slight smile forms across Kyle's mouth and then disappears. He sighs. "I'm gay, and I was kicked out of my church back home."

His words make me feel weak, the same feeling I get when I hear my son screaming from his bedroom or I read the Beatitudes.

"Oh man," I say, shaking my head, "I'm so sorry you were treated that way."

I want to get on a soapbox and rage against those who hurt him, like Sheryl Crow rages against people who use too much gasoline or Bruce Springsteen rages against pretty much everybody. But I know that won't make Kyle feel loved and accepted, just enraged. I also see that the countdown is down to fifty-six seconds. Jesus is less than a minute away.

"Kyle, if it means anything, I'm happy you came here this morning."

That's all I say. I want to gush about how much I love my church. I want to tell him that everybody is welcome here. I want to get on another soapbox about how God's story isn't limited by our own, but the timer's ticking down.

Three.

Two.

One.

The auditorium's lights go out. A video projection of a beautiful sunrise appears on a screen at the center of the stage. I glance at it quickly, but then I look back at Kyle. Music begins playing, and a chorus of ten drummers takes the stage, beating in unison as a young woman reads from Scripture about Mary Magdalene showing up at Jesus's tomb: *He is risen! Christ the Lord is risen.*

I pray. I ask God to give Kyle back his song. *Let him sing, God.*

And then the light show begins. It's a magnificent spectacle of pink, blue, purple, and green. To me, it looks like Rainbow Brite is puking on the church's stage. I close my eyes and try to sing about Jesus rising from the grave. Three songs into the praise and worship time, I look at Kyle. He's singing along at the top of his lungs. He looks over at me.

"I told you it was going to be a production," I say.

"It's *so* Nashville; I love it."

On the way out of church, Kyle asks if Margaret Becker goes to church here. I tell him no. He mouths an expletive and smiles. "But I'll still come back next Sunday."

I get into my car. At the first stoplight, I turn the radio on. I push the Seek button three times. Another church choir is singing "Christ the Lord Is Risen Today." I sing along. By the third verse, I'm singing as loud as I can. No light show. No production. Just me and a song and hope.

Acknowledgments

Thank you, Jessica, for loving me and believing in what I do. I love you "more than the sun." Elias, each and every day I am reminded how blessed I am to be your daddy. I love you, buddy.

Thank you, Mom and Dad, Melanie, Kelley, and Elisabeth, and their families. I love each of you so much.

Thank you, Rick and Debbie Schim, Melissa and Dan. It's an honor to be a part of your family.

Thank you, Shannon Marchese. Once again, I'm indebted to your editorial talent and willingness to push me out of my comfort zones. And thank you, Jessica Barnes, for lending your word skill to my stories; your talent humbles me. To Ken Peterson and everyone else at WaterBrook Press and Random House, thank you. You guys are amazing, and I'm so happy that you allow me the opportunity to share my story.

Much love and gratitude to friends: Pete and Brandi Wilson, Adam Ellis, Todd and Angie Smith, Matthew and Alyson Costner, Lee and Traci Steffen, Julie Barber, Michael Bianchi, Nicci Hubert, Lisa Baker, Andrea Christian, Eric DeVries, Dave Senes, Mandy Flemming, Chris and Anne Jackson, Jason Boyett, Jon Acuff, Jennifer

Schuchmann, Kortland Fuqua, Stephen Lamb, Greg Daniel, and the baristas at the Bellevue Starbucks.

And to you, the reader, thank you. All of this hard work would be pointless without you. Never let me forget that.

Peace, Matthew

www.MatthewPaulTurner.com

Follow Matthew on Twitter, at Twitter.com/JesusNeedsNewPR

Seven: An Excerpt from
Matthew Paul Turner's *Churched*

Fundamentalism made me weird.

I wasn't alone. It made lots of people weird. But I think some people at my church believed that was the point, that somewhere in the Bible, Jesus declared, "Blessed are the weird." Our weirdness was a form of obedience unto God.

Things got peculiar for me early on. One Sunday morning my friend Jenny waltzed into our third-grade Sunday school class carrying a large, red and green plaid tin her mother had decorated with a fluorescent pink bow.

"Guess what, Matthew?" Jenny took off her puffy white church coat and threw it on the table in front of her. "Today's my birthday, and since it's on a Sunday, and my mother hates having birthday parties on Sundays, she made cookies for everybody in our class instead. Want to see them?"

Before I could say yes, Jenny tore off the bow and opened the lid. I looked inside.

"Oh, wow, Jenny," I said. "Your mom made cookies that look like Jesus."

Jenny's mother could make almost anything look like Jesus. Jenny brought most of her creations into school for show and tell. Her mother was best known for making Jesus-shaped throw pillows. Jenny told the class it was her mother's spiritual gift to take something not *naturally* about Jesus and come up with a creative way to make it artificially about him.

My mother did the same thing when she got the bright idea to throw Jesus a birthday party on Christmas Eve one year. In preparation for Jesus's birthday bash, Mom made a cake and put thirty-three birthday candles in it. After our church's Christmas Eve service, we came home and gathered around our dining-room table, lit the candles, and sang "Happy Birthday" to God's only Son.

After we finished singing, we stood really still and stared at the birthday cake for a couple of seconds. I think we were waiting to see who would blow out the candles, wondering if a mighty rushing wind would blow through the house and extinguish the flames.

Nothing happened.

Eventually, my brother-in-law leaned in and blew out the candles. Then he looked at all of us and said, "What? I didn't do anything."

The party wasn't as exciting as the Day of Pentecost, but the cake was good, and Mom was proud of herself, which was what being fundamentalist was all about. Pride went before a fall, but it was also something comfortable to lean on once in a while.

It was difficult to look at Jenny's Jesus-shaped cookies without wanting to pick one up so I could smell his face. I had never seen the face of Jesus look delicious before. I'd seen it look peaceful, patient, happy, and once even angry. But I'd never craved it with milk.

"Don't they look yummy?" Jenny asked. "Mom found Jesus cookie cutters in a Christian catalog." Jenny placed the lid back on the tin to keep her Jesus snacks from getting stale. "The frosting is homemade, but Mom had a hard time making the color brown, so his hair looks a little purple."

Now that she mentioned it, the cookies did resemble Tina Turner more than Jesus.

"Jenny, do you think Mrs. Snover will let us eat Jesus?"

I wasn't trying to be a downer, but I worried that it might be against our religion to digest the Son of God.

"Daddy wondered the same thing," said Jenny, "but Mom was like, 'Oh don't worry about it, hon! I used to be Catholic, and we ate Jesus all the time during communion.'"

My eyes widened. "Catholics *eat* Jesus?"

"That's what Mom said."

"That's disgusting. I'm happy I'm Baptist. I don't want to eat Jesus every Sunday."

When Mrs. Snover finished teaching us about Jesus's miracle of turning water into Welch's grape juice, the whole class sang "Happy Birthday" to Jenny, and I bit into Jesus's cheekbone.

He tasted good. So good that I saved some of his crumbs in a napkin just in case he wanted to come back to life in my pocket.

He spent his childhood trapped within the confines
of countless bizarre, strict rules.

And lived to tell about it.

Matthew Paul Turner shares amusing, sometimes cringe-worthy,
and poignant stories about growing up in a fundamentalist house-
hold, where even well-intentioned contemporary Christian music
was proclaimed to be "of the devil."

churched is a collection of stories that detail one American boy's
experiences in the confines of strict religion. Yet despite all that, he
grew into a man who, amidst the chaotic mess of religion, falls in
love with Jesus.

WATERBROOK PRESS
www.waterbrookmultnomah.com